ABOUT THIS BOOK

Exams are about much more than just repeating memorised facts, so we have planned this book to make your revision as active and effective as possible.

How?

- by breaking down the content into manageable chunks (Revision Sessions)

- by testing your understanding at every step of the way (Check Yourself Questions)

- by highlighting key words and definitions you MUST know (e.g. **health**, **hygiene**)

- by listing the most likely exam questions for each topic (Question Spotters)

- by giving you invaluable examiner's guidance about exam technique (Exam Practice)

REVISION SESSION 1

Revision Sessions

- Each Unit is divided into a number of short revision sessions. You should be able to read through each of these in no more than 30 minutes. That is the maximum amount of time that you should spend on revising without taking a short break.

- Ask your teacher for a copy of your own exam board's GCSE Physical Education specification. Tick off on the Contents list each of the revision sessions that you need to cover. It will probably be most of them.

CHECK YOURSELF QUESTIONS

- At the end of each revision session there are some Check Yourself Questions. By trying these questions, you will immediately find out whether you have understood and remembered what you have read in the revision session. Answers are at the back of the book, along with extra hints and guidance.

- If you manage to answer all the Check Yourself questions for a session correctly, then you can confidently tick off this topic in the 'Revised & understood' box provided in the Contents list. If not, you will need to tick the 'Revise again' box to remind yourself to return to this topic later in your revision programme.

RevisionGuide

GCSE Physical Education / Games

Kirk Bizley

Series editor: Jayne de Courcy

SPORT ENGLAND

A javelin is clearly a potentially dangerous object to throw.

CONTENTS AND REVISION PLANNER

QUESTION SPOTTER

It's obviously important to revise the facts, but it's also helpful to know how you might need to use this information in your exam.

The author, who has been involved with examining for many years, knows the sorts of questions that are most likely to be asked on each topic. He has put together these Question Spotter boxes so that they can help you to focus your revision.

Key Words and Definitions

Throughout the book, the subject-specific words that you need to understand in exam questions and use in your answers are highlighted clearly, e.g. **flexibility**. If it is a term that you may need to define in your exam, then the definition is pulled out in coloured text, e.g. '**flexibility** is defined as the range of movement around a joint'.

The glossary at the end of the book contains all the key words so that you can double-check that you know them all.

Exam Practice

■ This Unit gives you invaluable guidance on how to answer exam questions well.

■ It contains some sample students' answers to typical exam questions, followed by examiner's comments on them showing where the students gained and lost marks. Reading through these will help you get a very clear idea of what you need to do in order to score full marks when answering questions in your GCSE Physical Education exam.

■ There are also a number of typical exam questions for you to try answering. Model answers are given at the back of the book for you to check your own answers against.

■ Working through this unit will give you an excellent grounding in exam technique.

About your GCSE Physical Education/Games course

Does this book match my course?

This book has been written to match **all of the Physical Education and Physical Education/Games GCSE specifications** produced by the three exam boards in England. Two of the boards, AQA and OCR, offer the PE/Games option as well as the Physical Education award so you should ask your teacher to make sure you know exactly which exam you will be taking.

If possible, get hold of a copy of your own exam board's specification and mark off the topics you need to revise on the contents list at the front of this book.

Revision sessions which only apply to one or two Boards' specifications are clearly marked in the book.

What will my exam questions be like?

Each exam board has a different format of paper with different types of questions:

- AQA Specification A has compulsory sets of structured questions with different sections to each question. There is an increase of difficulty within each question, with the most difficult part at the end.

- AQA Specification B has compulsory sets of structured questions with different sections to each question. There is an incline of difficulty within each question with most difficult part at the end. There is also a section with a choice of questions and in this section there are extended writing (essay type) answers required.

- Edexcel has a paper that is divided into three parts. Part I has multiple-choice questions, Part II has short answer questions and Part III has scenario questions.

- OCR has short answer questions, and structured questions that increase in difficulty.

The Exam Practice section in this book (pages 126-140) has examples of all these different sorts of questions. When practising answering questions, you should stick to the format of questioning which your particular exam board uses and get used to that format.

The practical component

All of the specifications have a practical component as well as a theory one and, although they are similar, there are slight differences between them.

The format for the four specifications is as follows:

- **AQA Specification A** - the practical coursework for this is worth 60% of the total marks. You will be assessed on four different physical activities and you will also have to plan an exercise training programme linked to a specific physical activity or game.

- **AQA Specification B** – the practical coursework for this accounts for 50% of your total marks. You will be assessed on four different physical activities and an analytical investigation.

- **Edexcel** – the practical coursework for this is worth 60% of the total marks. You will be assessed on four different physical activities with an analysis of performance for one of the activities.

- **OCR** – the practical coursework for this is worth 60% of the marks. You will be assessed on four physical activities with an analysis of performance of one of the chosen activities under applied conditions.

The activities that are acceptable vary among the four boards, so you will be told by your teacher which ones you are able to put forward for assessment.

UNIT 1: HEALTH AND HYGIENE

■ Health ■

■ **Health** has a very clear definition, which was first used by the World Health Organisation:

Health is a state of complete physical, mental and social well–being and not merely the absence of illness or disease.

💡 **QUESTION SPOTTER**

Learning the definition of health is crucial: it will help you to answer questions in your exam.

🎾 Factors affecting your health

The following nine factors can influence your health:

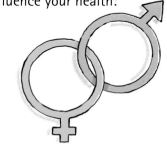

1 Use and abuse of substances – such as alcohol, tobacco, medicines and drugs.

2 Sex education – personal relationships, responsible attitudes and appropriate behaviour.

3 Family life – the contribution that living within a 'family' group can make to the development of attachments and concern and caring for others.

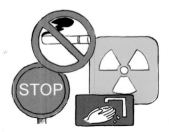

4 Safety – in different environments, at home, on the road, at school, at work, during leisure.

5 Health-related exercise.

6 Nutrition – the importance of a healthy diet, correct food preparation and handling rules.

7 Personal hygiene – cleanliness, avoiding disease.

8 Environmental aspects.

9 Psychological aspects – good mental health, avoidance of stress.

These factors may affect:
- your physical well-being
- your mental well-being
- your social well-being.

⚕ Effects of alcohol abuse

- The abuse of alcohol can seriously affect people's long-term health, as this diagram shows:

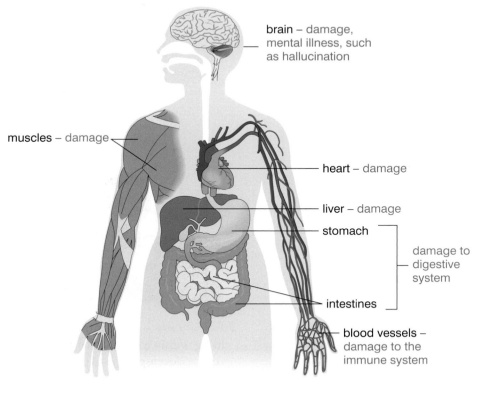

brain – damage, mental illness, such as hallucination

muscles – damage

heart – damage

liver – damage

stomach

damage to digestive system

intestines

blood vessels – damage to the immune system

- In the short term, too much alcohol can result in:
  - drunkenness
  - vomiting
  - lack of co-ordination and lack of balance
  - slowing down of reactions.

⚕ Effects of smoking

- Smoking can contribute to many diseases, as this diagram shows:

- Smoking is so bad for you that every packet carries this warning:

Smoking kills

- Another problem is that smokers can endanger other people through passive smoking.

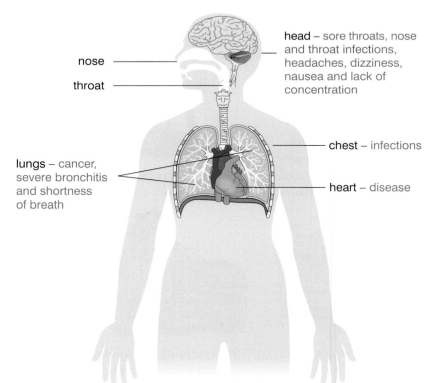

nose

throat

head – sore throats, nose and throat infections, headaches, dizziness, nausea and lack of concentration

chest – infections

lungs – cancer, severe bronchitis and shortness of breath

heart – disease

✎ Environmental factors

■ All the following have an effect on people's health:

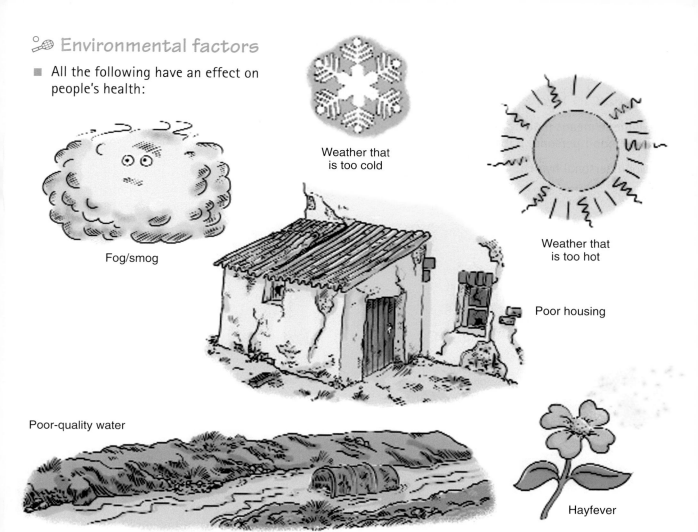

Weather that is too cold

Fog/smog

Weather that is too hot

Poor housing

Poor-quality water

Hayfever

✎ Medicines

■ Medicines are widely available and can cure many illnesses or aid recovery. They range from headache pills and cough medicines that you can buy over the counter to prescription medicines that have to be obtained from your doctor for complaints such as asthma.

✎ Immunisation

■ Immunisation is usually carried out through injection during childhood. It protects you from catching certain diseases such as tetanus, polio, measles and mumps. You can have special immunisations if you are travelling abroad to protect you against tropical diseases such as typhoid and diphtheria.

CHECK YOURSELF QUESTIONS

Q1 Give a simple definition of good health.

Q2 List some of the harmful effects of drinking too much alcohol.

Q3 What do you consider to be the MOST harmful effects of regular smoking?

Q4 Why is immunisation a good idea?

Answers are on page 141.

Hygiene

⌕ What is hygiene?

■ **Hygiene** means making sure you are clean and healthy, and have good personal habits, to stop the spread of germs.

Good personal hygiene includes the following nine factors:

1 Self-esteem and confidence

2 Washing-yourself and clothing

3 Cleaning – anything you come into contact with

4 Social considerations, e.g. body odour!

5 Prevention of disease

6 Clothing – clean and appropriate

7 Dental care

8 Good food preparation

9 Prevention of infection

🏸 Problems caused by poor hygiene

■ Not paying attention to good personal hygiene may result in some of these problems:

- **Athlete's foot** – a fungal infection between the toes, usually caused by not drying the feet properly.

- **Ingrown toe nails** – caused by not cutting toe nails properly/regularly.

- **Blisters** – caused by constant rubbing, often by incorrectly fitting footwear.

- **Corns** – a painful area of thickened skin on the toes or foot, caused by pressure.

- **Verrucas** – technically known as plantar warts, they are contagious warts on the sole of the foot.

QUESTION SPOTTER

You may be asked to identify and explain a problem caused by lack of hygiene – athlete's foot is a good example to choose.

? CHECK YOURSELF QUESTIONS

Q1 Why is making sure you have good hygiene habits going to help you to stay healthy?

Q2 Taking care of your feet is clearly important – describe two problems that could be caused by not taking hygiene precautions. How could these problems affect your effectiveness as a sports performer?

Answers are on page 141.

UNIT 2: NUTRITION AND DIET

Basic nutritional needs

Definition of nutrients

- **Nutrients** are the substances that make up food.

A balanced diet

- In order for our bodies to function normally, we all need to have a balanced, healthy diet – one that consists of the right mix of different types of food.

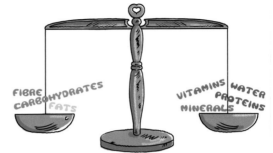

All these need to be present for a healthy, balanced diet.

Carbohydrates

- There are two basic categories of carbohydrate, simple and complex:

Simple carbohydrates are found in foods such as sugar, milk and fruit.

Complex carbohydrates are found in foods such as bread, pasta, potatoes, rice and pulses/beans.

- Carbohydrates are the main suppliers of energy to the body. They are stored as **glycogen** in the liver and muscles. Glycogen can be used to provide energy during exercise.

- Endurance athletes and performers often **carbo-load** (also known as **carbohydrate loading**) as a way of preparing themselves for a particular event or competition, in order to increase their energy levels.

QUESTION SPOTTER

A common question is 'What is carbohydrate loading and when and why would it be used by a performer?'

Fats

- Fats are a source of energy for the body. They also help to insulate the body and to keep the body temperature at the right level.

- Everyone has to control the amount of fat in their diet because too much fat can be the main cause of gaining overall body weight.

There are three main types of fats: saturates, mono-unsaturates and polyunsaturates. Fats are found in many foods, including cheese, cream, meat and cooking oils, butter and margarine.

Proteins

- Proteins are often known as 'building blocks', because they are so important in the growth of new tissue. When digested, they go into the blood stream as **amino acids**.

- Proteins are obtained from two sources, animals and vegetables:

Animal protein comes from fish, chicken and red meat.

Vegetable protein comes from pulses (beans) and grains. Foods produced from animal products, such as eggs, milk and cheese, also contain protein.

- Everybody needs to make sure that they have enough proteins but you might need more if you train hard or for long periods.

Vitamins

- Vitamins are essential to enable you to maintain good health. We need them in only small quantities and they are usually contained in a normal balanced diet.

- As each vitamin was discovered, it was given a letter. The basic ones are:

QUESTION SPOTTER

You do not need to know details of all of these vitamins for all exams. For AQA you need to know only about A, C and D and for Edexcel about A, B, C and E. For OCR you need to know about A, B, C, D, E and K.

- A deficiency of some vitamins can cause particular problems. A lack of vitamin C can cause scurvy and a lack of vitamin D can cause rickets.

Minerals

- Like vitamins, minerals are needed only in small amounts and we receive them mainly through eating vegetables and meats.

- The most common ones are:

QUESTION SPOTTER

You need to know about iodine, iron and calcium for AQA and about calcium and iron for Edexcel. For OCR you need to know about sodium as well!

Calcium	Sodium	Iron	Iodine
For bones and teeth	To maintain body fluids	For the transport of oxygen by red blood cells	For hormone formation, notably from the thyroid gland

Fibre/roughage

- Fibre is important as it aids the digestive system and also adds some bulk to food. It is contained in wholegrain cereals, wholegrain bread, oats, fruits and vegetables.

Water

- The human body is mostly water (about 70%) and on average we lose about 2.5 litres of water from our bodies every day. Water is also a means of transport for nutrients, waste and hormones.

- Failure to replace water can lead to **dehydration**, which can cause serious problems, such as heat exhaustion. It is important to replace the water you lose by drinking. If you fail to do so, your body will weaken to the point where it will stop functioning.

- The following will affect how quickly water is lost.

  - The intensity of any work or exercise being carried out.

  - The amount of time spent exercising.

  - The temperature and humidity of your environment.

QUESTION SPOTTER

Questions on dehydration are very common so it is important to know what it is and how to avoid it.

Water loss is always greater when you are exercising.

CHECK YOURSELF QUESTIONS

Q1 Give the seven basic components of a healthy, balanced diet.

Q2 Name the two types of carbohydrates and the three types of fats.

Q3 What is glycogen? Why would it be important to you in a sporting situation?

Q4 Why do the organisers of marathon races place water stations at regular intervals along the route?

Answers are on page 141.

Specific diets for performers

- Everyone needs to have a healthy diet, but some sports performers may need to make additions to their diet to make them more effective in their particular sport or activity.

A female gymnast needs to be small and light and so needs to avoid too much fatty food.

A weightlifter needs to be quite large and bulky and so additional fats and proteins may be needed.

A soccer player has to make sure that he has sufficient energy-providing food for a ninety minute game.

A marathon runner may have a high carbohydrate diet and specifically carbo-load for several days just before a race. He or she may even have specifically organised pasta parties to help them!

QUESTION SPOTTER

If you get a question asking you generally about any performer who might require a specific diet, then a marathon runner is the best one to choose!

- Age is also a factor in relation to diet. Younger people have periods of rapid growth where they may need a greater amount of food. As they get older this demand decreases and levels out.

- As you get older there is also often a need to regulate intake more carefully to avoid gaining too much weight.

Energy and activity

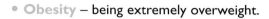

- The amount of activity you are undertaking will be a factor to consider in terms of diet. You also need some energy just to keep your body working at rest.

- Your **basal metabolic rate** is the amount of energy needed for important processes such as breathing and keeping the heart beating.

- If you do not balance your intake and output you can suffer from one of the following.

  - Obesity – being extremely overweight.

  - Anorexia – being extremely underweight.

  - Malnutrition – extreme weight loss.

QUESTION SPOTTER

You may be asked to give an example of a problem that can arise as the result of not having a balanced diet – obesity is a good example.

When to eat

What you take in must equal what you use.

LEEDS METROPOLITAN UNIVERSITY LIBRARY

- When you eat is also an important factor and you should take into account the following:

  - **Before activity** – do not eat too close to taking part in physical activity. Wait at least two hours after eating.

  - **During activity** – generally you should not eat during activity, although small quantities, e.g. fruit such as bananas, is all right.

  - **After activity** – leave the same two hour gap after activity before eating substantial amounts. However, drinking liquids straight away is a good thing, although drinking too much too quickly can make you feel uncomfortable.

- Remember that planning a diet for a sports performer is very much a long-term exercise and must be carried out over a substantial period of time.

CHECK YOURSELF QUESTIONS

Q1 For the following two specific diets, identify the type of sport each would be most appropriate for:
Diet 1: Plenty of carbohydrates, including attending a pasta party and carbo-loading just before an event.
Diet 2: Avoiding too many fatty foods in order to keep body weight regulated but ensuring that enough proteins and

carbohydrates are included to maintain energy levels.

Q2 Identify and describe a problem that could be caused by not having a balanced diet.

Q3 When would it be advisable for you not to eat large quantities of food? Why?

Answers are on page 141.

UNIT 3: HEALTH-RELATED EXERCISE

General fitness and exercise

Carrying out everyday activities requires you to be generally fit.

Why exercise?

- To be generally fit, you need to be in good health and able to carry out everyday tasks comfortably.

- **Exercise** can be defined as healthy physical exertion. Exercising regularly can benefit you in the following ways:

  - Improves your body shape

  - Helps to release stress and tension

  - Helps you to sleep better

  - Reduces the chances of getting illnesses and diseases

  - Gives you a physical challenge to aim for

  - Tones the body and the muscles, which can lead to better posture

  - Increases your basic levels of strength, stamina and flexibility.

- The amount of exercise you should carry out depends on your basic physical condition and your long-term aims.

- It is very easy to start some good exercise habits, such as:

  - Don't drive, or be driven, short distances but walk instead

  - Try to walk at least part of a journey – very easy to do if you travel by bus

  - Use a bicycle

  - Walk up stairs rather than use a lift

  - Do some simple stretching or flexibility exercises daily.

Exercise guidelines

- You need to think about the amount of exercise you should be taking. The following are some general guides.

  - Being slightly breathless after exercise is not a bad sign – but if you can't talk you have overdone it!

  - Try to exercise for periods of about 15–20 minutes four or five times a week.

- Exercise until you are pleasantly tired – do not overdo it.

- Go for all-round exercise such as swimming which is particularly good as it includes some stretching movements. Try to make regular exercise a routine – joining a club can help with this.

You shouldn't overdo exercise – but it should leave you feeling a bit tired...

Effects of exercise

■ The long-term effect of exercising is that you enjoy all the benefits listed on the previous page! There are also some short-term effects:

- The rate at which your heart beats will go up (your **pulse rate**).

- Your rate of breathing will increase.

- Your body temperature will increase and sweat will appear on the surface of your skin.

- Skin will appear to redden, especially on your face. You may have a feeling of tiredness or 'heaviness' in some of your muscles.

■ Someone who does not exercise regularly will find that when they do exercise they become breathless and tire quickly.

QUESTION SPOTTER

You may be asked a question about why you need to exercise and the effects that exercising regularly will have.

? CHECK YOURSELF QUESTIONS

Q1 Which plus points of exercising do you think are the most valuable?

Q2 How can you increase the amount of exercise that you take?

Q3 When you exercise, which effects do you notice most?

Answers are on page 142.

Physical activity

- Exercise is physical activity that improves health and fitness. It is for this reason that schools provide an HRE (health-related exercise) programme as part of their PE timetable.

- Within this programme there are five identifiable areas which are combined:

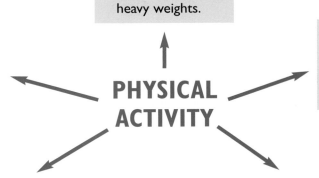

2 Muscular strength is our ability to lift heavy weights.

1 Cardiovascular fitness is our circulatory and respiratory systems working effectively together.

3 Muscular endurance is the ability of a muscle or group of muscles to keep working against a resistance.

PHYSICAL ACTIVITY

5 Body composition is the percentage of our body weight that is fat, muscle and bone.

4 Flexibility is our ability to have a good range of movement in our joints.

- Factors 1–4 are dealt with in more detail, specifically related to fitness, in Unit 4.

- Body composition can be divided into two categories:

  - **Body fat** – the percentage of your body fat.

  - **Lean body mass** – the total mass of your bones, muscles, connective tissue and body organs.

- Weighing yourself on the scales does not give you information on your body fat. It is possible to measure your body fat, however, through taking measurements of skinfolds at three specific points on the body:

  - **Biceps and triceps** – on the front and back of your upper arm.

  - Just below your shoulder blade (**subscapula**).

  - just above your hip bone at the front (**supra-iliac**).

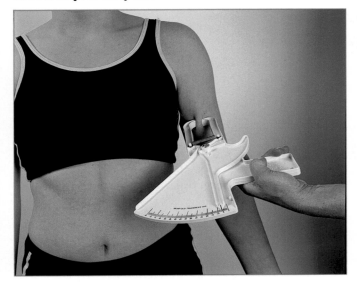

A skinfold measurement assesses your body fat.

- An important factor to do with body composition is your weight. Factors also linked to this include:

  - **Your age** – it is difficult to compare your height to weight ratio when you are growing rapidly. This is why there are no charts produced for young people.

  - **Your frame** – there are recognised frame sizes of small, medium and large. Your frame size can be worked out using measurements taken around your wrist.

  - **Your sex** – there are different weight charts for males and females because of the recognised differences between the two.

- There are charts that show a range of acceptable weights for men and women. Remember that for some physical activities, people may need to be bigger. A very active rugby player, for example, may choose to be bigger so that he or she can use his or her body size to advantage.

QUESTION SPOTTER

You need to be able to make the important distinction between body composition and body weight as this may form the basis of a question.

Being large does not mean that you cannot also be fit and healthy.

CHECK YOURSELF QUESTIONS

Q1 Why do you think schools have a health-related exercise programme?

Q2 Describe exactly what is meant by body composition.

Q3 What are the main factors that affect your own personal body composition?

Answers are on page 142.

REVISION
SESSION 3 ■ Specific fitness ■

- You can achieve specific fitness only if you have a good level of general fitness to start with.

- Specific fitness involves preparing for the particular demands of activities you are taking part in, which may often be at quite a high level. You may have high levels of natural ability and skill but these will not be enough – specific fitness will be essential.

- You will have to make sure you have regular training sessions relating to the following factors:

Strength Flexibility Endurance

SPECIFIC FITNESS TRAINING

Agility Speed

Flexibility is important to this gymnast and endurance is important to this distance runner.

- You might have to train to develop all of these factors, or you might decide to concentrate on some more than others. It will depend on the activity you are undertaking.

■ Achieving specific fitness is difficult and hard. It can also be affected by these factors:

- **Physical handicap** – can often be overcome by using adapted training equipment but there may be some restrictions on the numbers and types of activity that are accessible.

- **Illness** – can include broken bones, colds and 'flu. There could be temporary medical conditions or more permanent ones such as asthma.

- **Diet** – may have to be carefully controlled.

- **Drugs** – including alcohol and tobacco – will need to be limited.

- **Weight**, **height** and somatotype (your body type).

- **Mental stress** and **pressure of competition** at higher levels.

Illness can affect your fitness levels.

CHECK YOURSELF QUESTIONS

Q1 Explain the difference between being generally fit and specifically fit.

Q2 For all the factors listed above, list the ones you can do something about and the ones you have no control over.

Q3 Explain how you would go about getting specifically fit for running a marathon.

Answers are on page 142.

Unit 4: Components of Fitness

REVISION SESSION 1 ■ What is fitness? ■

■ **Fitness** can be defined as having a highly efficient body that can cope with a high level of physical demand.

■ The various components that combine in order to make you fit can be divided into two categories:

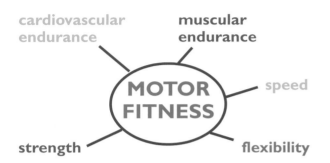

cardiovascular endurance | muscular endurance | speed | strength | flexibility

MOTOR FITNESS

agility | balance | co-ordination | reaction time | timing

SKILL-RELATED FITNESS

Motor fitness: you probably need elements of all of these components to be successful in sport, although some may be more important than others.

Skill-related fitness: you may find that you want to concentrate on particular components for particular sports or activities.

QUESTION SPOTTER

You may be asked to name particular components of fitness – it is *essential* that you know them all!

■ You do not have total control over all of the components listed above but you can work towards improving many of them. Remember too that you can be healthy without being fit but you cannot be fit without being healthy.

? CHECK YOURSELF QUESTIONS

Q1 Complete the name for all the following components of fitness and then put them into the correct column.

C ....   E.........
M ....   E.........
Sp.........
St ....
F ....
A ....
B ....
C ....
R ....   T.........
T ....

Motor fitness	Skill-related fitness

Answers are on page 142.

- Endurance can be divided into two categories: cardiovascular endurance and muscular endurance.

Cardiovascular endurance

- **Cardiovascular endurance** is the ability of the heart and lungs to keep supplying oxygen in the bloodstream to provide the energy to carry on with physical movement.

- The following effects occur in your body when you train or exercise strenuously:

  - The 'normal' heart rate of 72 beats per minute increases greatly.

  - The 'normal' breathing rate of 14–16 breaths per minute increases greatly.

  - The cardiac output (blood pumped from the heart) of approximately five litres per minute can increase by seven or eight times!

- Performers with good levels of cardiovascular endurance have the following:

  - A relatively slow resting heart rate – below half the normal rate is quite common.

  - A quicker recovery rate – this is the speed at which the heart rate returns to normal.

Cross-country runners needs a high level of cardiovascular endurance.

- Knowing how to find, locate and record your heart rate (pulse rate) is important. Your pulse is located:

  - On the side of your neck (the carotid pulse)

  - On the inside of the wrist (the radial pulse)

  - Just over the temple at the side of the forehead (the temporal pulse)

  - In the groin (the femoral pulse)

Locating the radial pulse at the wrist.

- In order to improve your levels of cardiovascular endurance, you need to train the body at certain levels.

Your pulse rate should be within these target zones.

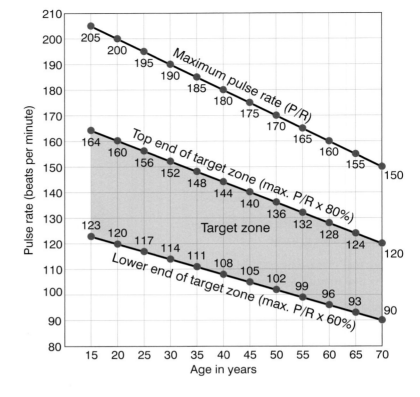

QUESTION SPOTTER

Knowing the significance of these training levels is very important as various questions may be based on them.

- Using the graph you can work out the following:

  - **Maximum pulse** – this can be worked out as 220 minus your age, so for a 15-year-old it would be 220 – 15 = 205.

  - **Top end of training zone** – which is 80% of maximum, so for a 15-year-old it would be 205 x 80% = 164.

  - **Bottom end of training zone** – which is 60% of maximum, so for a 15-year-old it would be 205 x 60% = 123.

Remember you cannot exercise your heart in quite the same way you exercise other parts of your body!

- In order to improve your cardiovascular endurance, you would need to exercise, or train, at a fairly high level and keep your heart rate at that level for at least 15 minutes.

- The overall effects of having a more efficient cardiovascular system are:

  - The heart rate is slower

  - The heart does not have to work so hard to pump blood around the body

  - You can enjoy physical activity without tiring too quickly.

🎾 Muscular endurance

Muscular endurance is the ability of the muscles, or a group of muscles, to keep working against a resistance.

■ If you are taking part in any activity that requires you to sustain power for up to four or five minutes, you will need a high level of muscular endurance because your muscles will have to work repeatedly for the whole event.

🎾 Improving muscular endurance

■ Circuit training is a good way of improving levels of muscular endurance. Another good method is weight training (see Unit 9) because you have to work on improving **dynamic strength** – the ability to support your own body weight over a period of time.

■ If you are not able to sustain high levels of muscular endurance, then you are likely to suffer the effects of **muscular fatigue**. This is where the muscle is no longer able to work properly; it will literally not be able to work against, or hold, a load any longer.

A climber needs a high level of muscular endurance.

? CHECK YOURSELF QUESTIONS

Q1 Define cardiovascular fitness.

Q2 What is the connection between your pulse rate and your level of cardiovascular endurance?

Q3 a If you hold your arms above your head for a long time, what type of endurance is needed?

b When you are no longer able to keep them there, what has occurred in your muscles?

Answers are on page 143.

Strength

- **Strength** is the maximum force that can be developed within a muscle or group of muscles during a single maximal contraction.

- There are different types of strength that may be used in different situations.

🎾 Types of strength

- **Static strength** is the greatest amount of strength that can be applied to an immovable object.

- **Dynamic strength** is the strength a person needs to sustain their body over a prolonged period of time, or to be able to apply some force against an object.

- **Explosive strength** is muscular strength used in one short, sharp movement.

These players have to use static strength to prevent them being moved.

This gymnast needs dynamic strength to complete this routine.

These sprinters use explosive strength to gain a good start.

QUESTION SPOTTER

You may be asked to name the different types of strength and to give an example of when each may be used.

- Remember that for most activities you will require a combination of all these forms of strength. It is not very often that you use only one of them.

Measuring strength

■ It is difficult to measure strength. Who is stronger: the small person who can perform 25 chin-ups or the large person who can lift a heavy weight? It is unlikely that either could match the other if they were to perform the other's task.

■ Some tests do exist. You can use a grip strength dynamometer which measures grip strength in the hand, and you can use a sergeant jump and standing broad jump to gauge leg strength.

Increasing strength

■ The most common method to increase strength is through weight training (see Unit 9) and it is relatively easy to work on increasing the strength of specific muscles, or muscle groups.

■ You can use either free-standing weights or specialist machines which allow you to exercise the muscles.

Using weights will increase upper body strength.

CHECK YOURSELF QUESTIONS

Q1 What is the basic definition of strength?

Q2 Define what is meant by the following:
a static strength
b explosive strength
c dynamic strength.

Q3 Why is it that strength is very specific to each individual, particularly in terms of their size?

Answers are on page 143.

Flexibility

QUESTION SPOTTER

This definition is one of the most common ones asked for in examination papers.

■ **Flexibility** is defined as the range of movement around a joint. Be aware that flexibility is sometimes also referred to as suppleness or even mobility.

Increasing flexibility

■ Increased flexibility may be achieved by regular stretching and getting the joints used to moving as far as possible. This has to be done gradually to allow the tendons, ligaments and muscles to adapt without any damage being caused.

This gymnast has developed an extreme range of flexibility.

■ The main joints involved in flexibility are:

- **Shoulders and arms** – obviously useful in throwing and swimming events.

- **Back** – a common area for problems to occur and very important for activities such as bowling in cricket.

- **Hips** – all bending movements require flexibility here so it would be essential for hurdlers.

- **Legs** – mainly in the knee and ankle joints, so any walking, running or kicking movement requires flexibility here.

Advantages of increased flexibility

- **Less chance of injury.** This is one of the main reasons why you include stretching exercises in a warm-up. If you try to stretch more than you are capable of then you are likely to damage a muscle.

- **Improved body posture.** This means that the muscles are holding the body in position correctly and none of the muscles are over-tight, which can cause aches and pains.

- **Better and improved performance.** There are some activities you simply cannot perform without a great deal of flexibility, notably gymnastics and hurdling.

- You might even be competing in something that awards marks for how well you can perform certain movements, so the better your flexibility the better the movements will look.

Testing flexibility

- The standard test for this is known as the 'sit and reach test'. To do this, you sit opposite a bench, or table, with your legs straight and you push against a slide to see how far you can move it. This specifically measures the flexibility of the lower back and hamstrings.

These hurdlers need a great deal of flexibility to perform their sport.

The 'sit and reach test' indicates how flexible you are.

CHECK YOURSELF QUESTIONS

Q1 Define flexibility.

Q2 Describe some basic stretching movements you might use to improve flexibility.

Q4 Why is it important to include some flexibility exercises in a warm-up?

Q4 Describe two sporting situations where an increased level of flexibility might be an advantage.

Answers are on page 143.

Speed, reaction time and power

🎾 Speed

- Speed is not just about how quickly you can run but also to do with how quickly you can perform a particular movement.

This discus thrower needs speed to be able to spin quickly.

- There are two factors that contribute to speed:

  - **Reaction time** is how quickly a performer can respond to something. For a sprinter this would be how quickly he or she could respond to the starting pistol at the start of a race.

  - **Movement time** is how quickly a performer can carry out a movement. For a sprinter, this would mean how quickly he or she can then run the race.

- The total speed would therefore be the combination of the reaction time and movement time.

🎾 Factors affecting speed

- It is possible to practise to improve speed but speed will also be affected by:

  - **Inherited factors** – many experts believe you are either born with speed or you are not. The number of fast twitch fibres (see Unit 6) is something you have naturally and cannot be altered.

  - **Body shape and size** – weight and muscle size might be changed but basic body shape cannot be altered.

  - **Duration and distance of the event** – it is not possible to maintain full levels of speed indefinitely. Distances up to 400 metres are considered to be sprint events and after that it is generally recognised that speed starts to decrease.

- Speed can, however, be increased by increasing strength, by developing your action and style (which improves your technique), and by making speed work part of your training programme.

Power

■ **Power** is defined as the combination of the maximum amount of speed with the maximum amount of strength.

■ There is a very strong link between power and explosive strength. Remember that power is not something that can be maintained over very long periods of time as it is used only in short bursts.

■ You do not necessarily have to be big and strong to generate power. Performers in racket sports such as badminton, squash and tennis have to generate power with their rackets for maximum effect.

■ Power is something you can work on when you are training. You can, for example, ensure that you add speed to lifts when you are weight training.

A powerful smash is essential for a top-level badminton player.

? CHECK YOURSELF QUESTIONS

Q1 What is meant by reaction time? Give an example of it from a sporting situation.

Q2 Which two factors combine to contribute to speed?

Q3 **a** What naturally occurring factors might affect the speed you can generate?
b What factors might you be able to work on to improve your speed?

Q4 Define exactly what power is a combination of.

Answers are on page 143.

Co-ordination, agility and balance

Co-ordination

- **Co-ordination** can be defined as the ability to use two or more body parts together.

- The body's movement system needs to be combined with its nervous system to produce co-ordinated movement. Instances of this include:

  - **Hand–eye co-ordination** – a tennis player needs this to be able to strike a ball.
  - **Foot–eye co-ordination** – a footballer needs this to kick a ball.
  - **Head–eye co-ordination** – any footballer heading a ball needs this.

- For good co-ordination you need to be able to control various body parts and limbs. Most people will find that they have better co-ordination on their dominant side, depending on whether they are right- or left-handed.

- The better your co-ordination, the better the standard of your performance will be.

A pole-vaulter needs a very high level of co-ordination for all the phases of his jump.

Agility

- **Agility** can be defined as a combination of flexibility and speed and the ability to change the position of the body quickly.

- Other expressions are often used to describe someone who is agile, including 'nimble' and 'fleet footed'. Be careful not to confuse 'agility' with 'flexibility' as they are not the same things. Being agile is a great advantage in many sporting situations.

QUESTION SPOTTER

You will often be asked questions regarding how being agile can make a performer more effective.

This gymnast requires great agility to perform her movements.

⚲ Balance

- **Balance** can be defined as the ability to retain the centre of mass (gravity) of the body above the base of support.

- Balance is something that the body tends to do automatically, but for many sports performers it is an essential factor in their performance.

- Being able to maintain balance also includes other factors such as:

  - **Strength** – static strength (see page 22) may be needed to maintain certain balances.

  - **Practice** – many balance movements require a great deal of practice before they are able to be performed consistently and well.

⚲ Types of balance

- There are two distinct types of balance:

  - **Static balance** – where the balance is a stationary one such as a handstand.

  - **Dynamic balance** – where there are changing conditions of movement or shape such as on the pommel horse.

Being able to maintain total balance is essential for gymnasts.

? CHECK YOURSELF QUESTIONS

Q1 If a left-handed tennis player tried to play tennis with his racquet in his right hand, how might this affect his co-ordination?

Q2 In which particular sport, or sporting activity, do you find you require the greatest levels of co-ordination?

Q3 Define agility.

Answers are on page 143.

UNIT 5: PHYSIOLOGICAL AND PSYCHOLOGICAL FACTORS

Physiological factors

⌦ Definition

- A **physiological factor** is one that affects your living body and therefore affects you physically.

⌦ Age

- Your age is an important physiological factor, whether you are young or old. Almost all sport at school is initially organised in age groups.

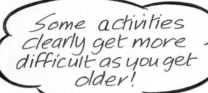

Some activities clearly get more difficult as you get older!

⌦ Reasons for age divisions

- **Practising and learning ability** – very young people cannot cope with difficult tasks, which is why sports are not introduced until they are older.

- **Flexibility** decreases with age, which therefore makes some activities, such as gymnastics, more difficult as you get older.

  - **Oxygen capacity** and **reaction time** decrease with age.

  - **Diet** needs to be adjusted as you get older as there is a tendency to put weight on.

  - **Injury** and **disease** are more common as you get older, bones become more brittle and recovery times are longer.

  - **Skill levels** start to increase as you get into your teens and twenties but may then start to decline as you get older.

  - **Strength**, like skill, starts to increase as you get older, peaking in the twenties and thirties but then decreasing as you enter your forties.

- There are many sports where it is generally accepted that younger people have an advantage, gymnastics being the main one. There are also activities where some age and experience are also advantageous, such as soccer, hockey and rugby.

⌦ Gender

- The anatomical differences between men and women mean that there are differences in their physical capabilities. GCSE Physical Education recognises these differences and makes allowances for them when practical activities are assessed.

Gender differences

- **Fat content** – women have a 30% greater fat content than men and this is considered to be an advantage in some endurance events.

- **Strength** – on average, women have only two-thirds the strength of men, which clearly disadvantages them in strength-based events.

- **Body type** – women have a flatter, broader pelvis, and smaller heart and lungs.

- **Flexibility** – women tend to be far more flexible than men.

■ In the past, there has been discrimination against women in sport. It is only comparatively recently that women have been allowed to compete in marathons and some of the long-distance running events. Some activities, such as dance and gymnastics, are sometimes thought to be 'unmanly'.

Disability

■ There are a great number of different disabilities, both mental and physical.

■ Sport for disabled people is now organised on a widespread basis. There are opportunities to play many activities, from wheelchair basketball to swimming events.

Access for those with disabilities

■ The law has been changed to make sport more accessible to all people with disabilities. There are now:

- wider parking bays

- ramp access for wheelchairs

- automatic doors

- special changing areas and toilets

- lifts and wider corridors.

QUESTION SPOTTER

Questions about the changing attitudes to women in sport are quite popular. They often ask for examples of where there has been an increase in women participating, such as marathon running and long-distance running events.

Wheelchair basketball is one of the fastest growing sports that disabled people take part in.

? CHECK YOURSELF QUESTIONS

Q1 In what sport is there an organised 'Seniors Tour' for the over-50s?

Q2 Name one sporting activity where men and women compete against each other on equal terms.

Q3 Name an activity where women may have a physiological advantage over men.

Answers are on page 144.

REVISION SESSION 2

Psychological factors

Definition

■ A **psychological factor** is one that affects, or arises in, the mind.

Stress

■ Stress is a state of mental strain and is linked to both anxiety and tension. Stress can improve or decrease the level of a performance, so it can be a positive or a negative factor.

■ To many performers, a moderate level of stress will spur them on to perform well, but if it is raised to a very high level, it is likely that the standard of a performance will go down. It is due to this that stress levels have to be controlled and managed in the following ways:

- By using mental rehearsal as a way of preparing for action. Sprinters often use this at the start of a race.

- Through encouragement and reassurance from team mates or coaches and trainers.

- By making targets reasonable in terms of what is expected from a performance.

- Through relaxation techniques – such techniques, which are often used by sport psychiatrists, who are becoming more common in all sports.

■ To experience stress is quite common. Top-level performers would worry if they did not experience it!

■ Stress in everyday life is thought of as a dangerous thing and can lead to illness. It is generally recognised that regularly taking part in sport can reduce stress levels and this is one of the reasons put forward for participating in sport.

A large crowd will often create a stressful situation for a performer.

QUESTION SPOTTER

You may well be asked how tension/anxiety/stress can affect a performance. Remember that stress is not always a bad thing in sport; it can have positive effects as well.

Motivation

- **Motivation** is the amount of determination a player has to do well. A highly motivated player is more likely to cope with anxiety, stress and tension because they are positive about what they are doing and they want to succeed.

- There are two forms of motivation:

  - Intrinsic motivation – comes from internal factors and personal reasons for wanting to do well. At a lower level of sport it can be as basic as just the enjoyment of taking part, keeping fit or setting some particular personal goals to achieve.

  - Extrinsic motivation – is more of an external factor and includes such things as winning trophies, prize money or the adulation and fame that comes from being a winner. The award schemes of a sport's governing bodies provide a form of extrinsic motivation.

- It can be difficult to remain motivated, which is one of the reasons why it is very difficult for top performers in any sport to stay at the top for very long. It is for this reason that many of them employ a personal coach to help and encourage them.

Examiners will often ask you to identify something that could be a motivating factor to assist an individual to be more successful in sport.

Intrinsic motivation is usually the reason dancers take part in their sport.

Arousal

- **Arousal** is the state of readiness of a performer. Motivation contributes to the level of arousal a performer achieves. Another term often used in association with arousal is 'psyching-up', which coaches and even captains may use before an event or competition in an effort to fully motivate players and competitors.

- One thing to be wary of is 'over-arousal', which can lead to poor sporting behaviour as a performer reaches such a state that they lose self-control. This is why too much 'psyching-up' is often considered to be a bad thing and is certainly not encouraged with young people.

CHECK YOURSELF QUESTIONS

Q1 Does stress improve or decrease the levels of a performance?

Q2 List three possible **intrinsic** motivating factors for someone playing social golf.

Q3 List three possible **extrinsic** motivating factors for someone playing club tennis.

Answers are on page 144.

The skeletal system

The functions of the skeletal system

- The skeletal system consists of the bones and joints of the body.

- There are five main functions of this system:

  1 **Support** – it keeps everything in our body in place and without a skeleton everything would collapse.

  2 **Shape** – it gives the overall shape and size of our bodies.

  3 **Movement** – this is achieved through the joints. The movement at the joints is known as articulation.

  4 **Protection** – all the vital organs of the body are protected by bones. For example, the heart and lungs are behind the ribs.

  5 **Blood cell production** – blood is made in the bone marrow.

Types of bones

- Bones are classified in four categories:

  1 **Long bones** – examples include the femur and the humerus.

  2 **Short bones** – examples include the carpels and phalanges.

  3 **Flat, or plate, bones** – examples include the ribs and sternum.

  4 **Irregular bones** – the main examples of these are the vertebrae in the back.

QUESTION SPOTTER

Being able to identify these five functions of the skeleton is essential.

QUESTION SPOTTER

Make sure you know an example of at least one bone for each type as questions about them are very common.

QUESTION SPOTTER

It is important to know not only the name of these bones, but also their location, because this is a popular topic. Study the labelled diagram opposite and memorise the bones you need to know *and* their location, for your exam board.

AQA Spec. A	OCR	Edexcel
Clavicle	Skull	Cranium (skull)
Scapula	Scapula	Sternum
Humerus	Clavicle	Ribs
Radius	Humerus	Ilium
Ulna	Sternum	Humerus
Sternum	Radius	Ulna
Ribs	Ulna	Radius
Pelvis	Ribs	Femur
Femur	Vertebrae	Patella
Tibia	Pelvis	Tibia
Fibula	Carpels	Fibula
Patella	Metacarpals	Scapula
	Phalanges	Clavicle
	Femur	Tarsals
	Patella	Metatarsals
	Tibia	Phalanges
	Fibula	Cervical vertebrae
	Tarsals	Thoracic vertebrae
	Metatarsals	Lumbar vertebrae
		Sacrum
		Coccyx

⊘ The main bones of the skeleton

- There are over 200 bones in the skeleton! You do not have to know them all but you do need to know the main ones. The diagram shows where they are located and the table on the previous page lists which ones you need to know for each exam board. Tick off the ones you need to know for your exam on the diagram.

⊘ Joints

- A **joint** is a place where two or more bones meet.

- There are over 100 joints in the body, and like the bones of the skeleton you do not have to learn them all – just the major ones!

⊘ Types of joint

- Joints can be classified into three main groups:

  1 **Immovable** – also known as fibrous or fixed – examples of these include the bones of the pelvis and those in the skull.

  2 **Slightly movable** – also known as cartilaginous – examples of these include the vertebrae in the spine.

  3 **Freely movable** – also known as synovial – these are the majority of the skeletal joints and come into separate categories such as:
     - **gliding** – examples include the joints between the small bones in the hands and feet
     - **hinge** – the two most common ones are the elbow and the knee
     - **pivot** – the main example is the joint at the top of the neck where the atlas and axis bones meet
     - **condyloid** – the best example is in the wrist
     - **ball and socket** – the two main examples are in the shoulder and the hip.

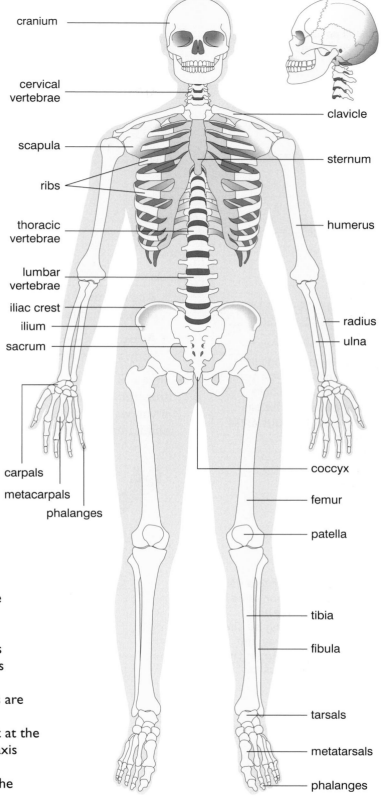

The main bones in the human skeleton.

The knee joint

The knee joint is a synovial hinge joint.

- The knee joint is the best example of a synovial hinge joint in the body and is also the largest and most complex of all the joints.

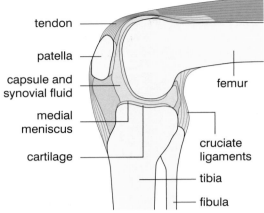

tendon
patella
capsule and synovial fluid
medial meniscus
cartilage
femur
cruciate ligaments
tibia
fibula

Types of movement

- Every movement that the body makes has a particular name. For example:

  - **Flexion** – this is when the angle between two bones is decreased, such as bending the arm at the elbow.

  - **Extension** – this is where the angle between two bones is increased, such as straightening the arm at the elbow.

  - **Rotation** – this is where the bone is able to move around in an arc, such as the arm at the shoulder.

  - **Abduction** – this is the movement of a bone or limb away from the body, such as raising the arm sideways from the body.

  - **Adduction** – this is the movement of a bone or limb towards the body, such as moving the arm back in towards the body sideways.

- Here is a useful way to learn the last two movements. When you add something it goes on to something, so adduction is moving **on** towards. If you were to abduct someone, you would be taking them away, so abduction is the moving **away** of the limb.

QUESTION SPOTTER

It is very common to have a question about the knee joint and even to have a diagram such as the one above which you are asked to label.

When doing a star jump, your arms and legs are abducting as they move away and adducting as they come back in.

QUESTION SPOTTER

Questions on the types of movement are common and usually ask for an example of the movement.

Joint structure and connective tissue

■ In order for joints to work effectively, they have to be joined and also protected. This is done by:

- **Cartilage** – this is shiny, smooth, slippery covering on the ends of the joint surfaces. It acts as a shock absorber and buffer and cushions against impact. Most people know of the cartilage in the knee as it is often damaged or injured.

- **Ligaments** – these are bands of fibres that are attached to the bones and link the joints together.

- **Tendons** – these are very strong cords that join the muscle to the bone.

QUESTION SPOTTER

Questions asking the difference between ligaments and tendons are often asked so make sure that you know the difference between the two.

Composition of bone

■ Bones are formed from cartilage that hardens into bone through the addition of calcium and other minerals. The actual bone growth begins in the centre of each bone. The process of development from cartilage to bone is known as **ossification**.

■ A balanced and healthy diet (see Unit 2) is needed to ensure that you have healthy bones and this should be combined with regular exercise.

QUESTION SPOTTER

Only the Edexcel exam board tests you on this.

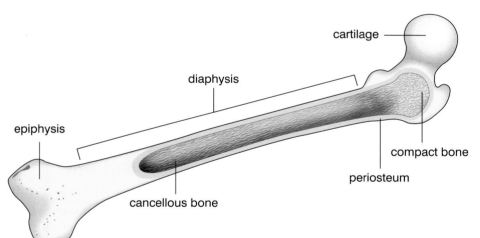

cartilage

diaphysis

epiphysis

compact bone

periosteum

cancellous bone

The different parts of bone.

CHECK YOURSELF QUESTIONS

Q1 What are the five functions of the skeleton?

Q2 What types of bone are the following?
  a femur
  b phalanges
  c ribs
  d vertebrae

Q3 What are the three types of joints known as?

Q4 What type of joint is the knee joint?

Q5 What is the difference between extension and flexion? Give an example of each movement.

Answers are on page 144.

The muscular system

Muscle types

■ There are three types of muscle:

- **Voluntary** or **skeletal** – all of these muscles are attached to the skeleton and they make up the majority of the muscles (see diagram on next page). They are under conscious control through the nervous system and move at will.

- **Involuntary** or **smooth** – these are muscles that you cannot control and that contract and relax automatically. They are found in the digestive and circulatory systems.

- **Cardiac** is a specific type of muscle that is found only in the wall of the heart. It is also an involuntary muscle as it is constantly contracting and relaxing as the heart beats.

Muscles and movement

■ The voluntary muscles enable movement. Remember that muscles can only **pull**; they do not push. It is because of this that muscles are arranged in pairs, so that one contracts (becomes smaller) while the other relaxes (becoming longer), and then the process reverses for the opposite movement.

■ The particular terms relating to movement are:

- **Antagonist** – the muscle that relaxes and lengthens.

- **Prime mover (agonist)** – the muscle that contracts and shortens.

- **Synergist** – the other muscles that also help in the movement and are sometimes known as the 'helper' muscles.

- **Origin** – the end of the muscle that is fixed to something rigid.

- **Insertion** – the end of the muscle that is fixed to the bone that moves.

QUESTION SPOTTER

It is very common to be asked what the three types of muscles are and also to give an example of each of them.

As the elbow bends (flexes), the bicep is the agonist, with the triceps the antagonist. As the elbow straightens (extends), the opposite occurs.

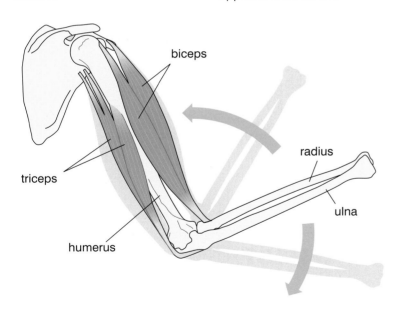

biceps

triceps

radius

ulna

humerus

The major skeletal muscles

■ There are more than 600 muscles in the body, but you do not have to learn them all! The diagram shows the major ones that you need to learn.

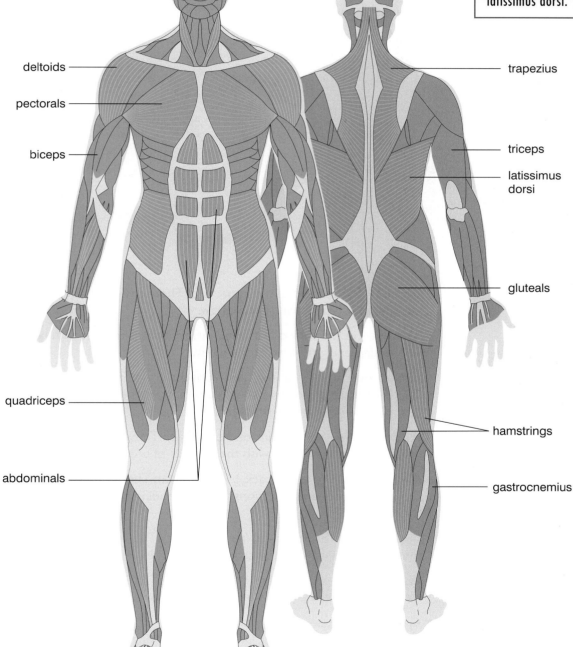

deltoids

pectorals

biceps

quadriceps

abdominals

trapezius

triceps

latissimus dorsi

gluteals

hamstrings

gastrocnemius

The skeletal muscles in the human body.

■ The specifically identified muscles all play an important part in particular actions or movements as follows:

- **Deltoids** – on the front and rear of the shoulder. These assist with raising and lowering the arm.

- **Trapezius** – by the neck and the upper back. These assist with shoulder movement and raising and lowering the neck.

- **Pectorals** – at the front of the upper chest. These assist with lifting or raising your arms, particularly above your head.

When you are doing a press-up, the majority of the movement is performed by the biceps and triceps.

- **Biceps** – at the front of the upper arm. These assist with bending and straightening of the arm at the elbow.

- **Triceps** – at the back of the upper arm. These also assist with bending and straightening the arm at the elbow.

- **Latissimus dorsi** – on the back from the armpit to the lower back. This is often referred to as 'the pulling muscle' as it allows a great deal of movement in the shoulders.

- **Abdominals** – at the front of the stomach. These allow bending at the waist and they also assist with the process of breathing.

- **Gluteals** – at the lower back, by the bottom. These assist with most of the walking and running actions and the bending and straightening of the legs.

- **Quadriceps** – at the upper front of the leg. This is a group of four muscles that assist with the straightening of the legs.

- **Hamstrings** – at the upper back of the leg. This is a group of three muscles that assist with the bending of the knee.

- **Gastrocnemius** – at the back bottom rear of the leg (calf). These assist with walking, running, jumping and pointing the toes.

QUESTION SPOTTER

You will often be asked to describe the exact location of a particular muscle and also to state what basic action it allows.

Muscle fibres

- There are two types of fibres present in voluntary muscle:

  - **Fast twitch fibres** – these are white and work quickly for short-term power and strength activities.

  - **Slow twitch fibres** – these are red with a good oxygen supply and contact slowly for long-term endurance activities and events.

- The levels of fast and slow twitch fibres in our bodies are hereditary, so no amount of training can affect the distribution of them.

- Obviously, a higher percentage of fast twitch fibres helps a sprinter and a higher percentage of slow twitch fibres helps a marathon runner. This explains why some people seem to be 'natural' sprinters with inherited speed, while others struggle to gain any more speed no matter how hard they might train.

Specialised medical tests can discover the levels of fast and slow twitch fibres.

CHECK YOURSELF QUESTIONS

Q1 Name the three different types of muscle.

Q2 What is the opposite type of movement to the prime mover, or agonist?

Q3 In the drawing (right) of the elbow, label the origin and the insertion for the bicep muscle.

Q4 Which type of muscle fibre would be most helpful to a cross-country skier and why would this be the case?

Q5 Complete the following table by naming the muscle from the location description.

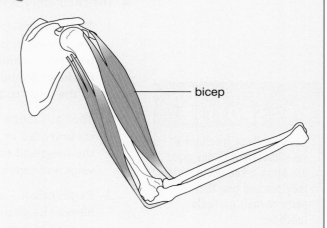

bicep

Location description	Name of muscle
The top, front of the upper arm	
By the neck, on the upper back	
The front of the upper chest	
At the lower back, by the bottom	
At the back, bottom, rear of the leg	
The upper front of the leg	

Answers are on page 144.

UNIT 7: THE CIRCULATORY AND RESPIRATORY SYSTEMS

REVISION SESSION 1 The circulatory system

QUESTION SPOTTER

All of the definitions are important. You might be asked to define one or more of the systems, but you might also be asked a question about how they particularly affect participation and performance.

- The **circulatory system** is defined as the heart and blood vessels that carry blood around the body.

- The **respiratory system** is defined as the organs of the body involved in the inhalation and expiration of air.

- The **cardiovascular system** is basically the circulatory and respiratory systems working together. It is defined as the circulation of blood and the transport of oxygen and nutrients to the cells of the body and waste products away from these cells.

- It is important to understand the ways in which these systems are interdependent as they work together in order to enable your body to work effectively, particularly during exercise or training.

Functions of the circulatory system

- The circulatory system has three main functions:

  1 **Transport** – this is how the blood, water, oxygen and nutrients are carried throughout the body and also how the waste is transported and removed. The blood transports oxygen from the lungs to the body's tissues and then carbon dioxide back to the lungs to be exhaled.

  2 **Temperature control and regulation** – the body temperature is controlled as the blood absorbs the body heat and carries it to the lungs and then to the skin, where it is released through the veins and capillaries.

  3 **Protection** – antibodies that fight infection are carried in the blood. The circulatory system also helps with the process of the clotting of blood to seal cuts and wounds.

QUESTION SPOTTER

Knowing these functions is very important as questions are often asked about what they are and how they perform their particular function.

Parts of the circulatory system

- There are three main parts of the circulatory system:

  1 the heart

  2 the blood

  3 the blood vessels.

✎ The heart

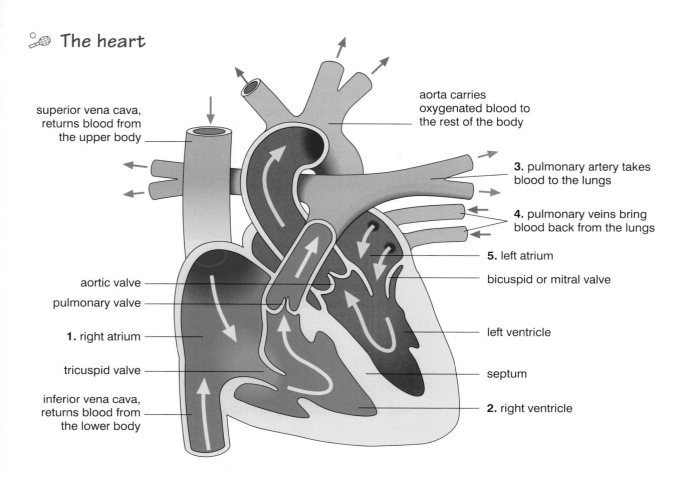

superior vena cava, returns blood from the upper body

aorta carries oxygenated blood to the rest of the body

3. pulmonary artery takes blood to the lungs

4. pulmonary veins bring blood back from the lungs

5. left atrium

bicuspid or mitral valve

aortic valve

pulmonary valve

1. right atrium

tricuspid valve

inferior vena cava, returns blood from the lower body

left ventricle

septum

2. right ventricle

■ The heart is basically a pump. It acts in the following way:

I Blood enters the right atrium. At this point it is dark red with little oxygen but mainly waste products such as carbon dioxide.

2 The right atrium pumps the blood into the right ventricle, through the tricuspid valve.

3 The right ventricle pumps the blood through the pulmonary artery to the lungs where oxygen is picked up and the carbon dioxide is deposited. It is at this point that the blood changes colour to bright red because of the oxygen it has collected.

4 From the lungs the blood returns to the left atrium through the pulmonary vein.

5 The left atrium pumps the blood into the left ventricle and the blood then leaves here through the aorta to be distributed to the rest of the body.

The blood

- Blood is made up of several different components:

  - **Red blood cells** – these carry oxygen to where the body needs it and they are extremely small. They are coloured red because they contain the pigment haemoglobin.

  - **White blood cells** – these are the body's main defence against infection and disease. They are not as plentiful as red blood cells. They are transparent cells in the blood plasma and some can produce antibodies that protect the body from infection.

  - **Platelets** – these help with blood clotting and are small fragments or particles of larger cells. They can help to seal the skin and also perform the same function on damaged blood vessels.

  - **Plasma** – this makes up the remaining 55% of the blood. It is a liquid mainly made up of water. It also contains fibrinogen, protein (to assist in clotting), nutrients such as glucose and some carbon dioxide and oxygen.

Blood vessels

- All the blood has to flow through blood vessels. These are:

  - **Arteries** – these have relatively thick walls and carry the blood at high pressure away from the heart. They have no valves and have more elastic walls than veins. They sub-divide into smaller vessels called arterioles.

  - **Veins** – these carry venous, or deoxygenated, blood back to the heart and they have thinner walls than arteries, which are also less elastic. Veins have valves to make sure that the blood is not able to flow backward through the vein.

  - **Capillaries** – these are microscopic vessels that link the arteries with the veins. They are very thin and allow carbon dioxide, oxygen, nutrients and waste products to pass through their walls.

The effect of exercise and training on the circulatory system

- The heart responds to increased levels of exercise by improving its efficiency and becoming stronger so that it pumps the blood around the body more efficiently. It actually becomes bigger, and highly trained performers have significantly larger hearts than average.

Benefits

- The following result from increased levels of training and exercise:

  - **Increased stroke volume** – this is the amount of blood that is pumped by the heart during one single beat. This can be considerably improved, whereby more oxygen is supplied to the working muscles.

- **Increased cardiac output** – this is how much blood the heart pumps out, so it is the total volume of blood pumped in one minute. If this is increased, it means that the respiratory and circulatory systems are working more efficiently and this helps greatly in endurance-type events.

- **Lower resting heart rate** – the average resting heart rate is between 60 and 80 (averaging for most adults at 72) beats per minute. This can be decreased to at least half this level with regular training.

A very common question will ask about the benefits which a performer gains from having a more efficient circulatory, respiratory or cardiovascular system. Remember that you will have to relate the benefits to the particular system and that many of them overlap.

Cycling over distance is one of the most effective ways of either exercising or training to increase the efficiency of the cardiovascular system.

CHECK YOURSELF QUESTIONS

Q1 Define the following:
   a the circulatory system
   b the respiratory system
   c the cardiovascular system

Q2 What are the three main functions of the circulatory system?

Q3 Through which blood vessel does the blood leave the heart to be distributed around the body?

Q4 What is the main function of the following?
   a red blood cells
   b white blood cells
   c platelets

Q5 What are the two main differences between veins and arteries?

Answers are on pages 144–5.

The respiratory system

■ The respiratory, or breathing, system consists of the following:

- **air passages**
- **lungs**
- **the mechanism of breathing**.

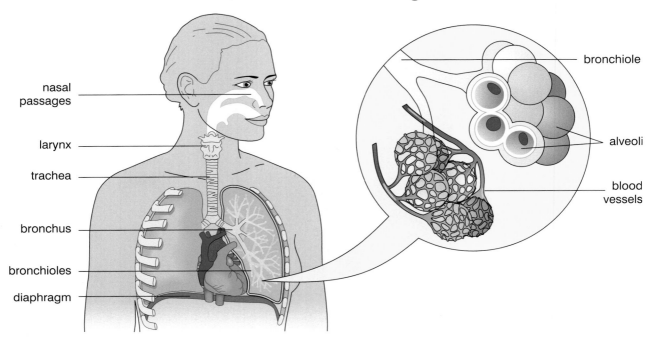

The respiratory system.

nasal passages

larynx

trachea

bronchus

bronchioles

diaphragm

bronchiole

alveoli

blood vessels

Air passages

■ The air passages consist of the following;

- **Nasal cavity** – the air enters here through the nostrils.

- **Mouth** – air also enters through here but is separated from the nostrils by the palate and it is this that allows you to chew food and breathe at the same time.

- **Pharynx** – this allows the food and air to enter. The air goes through the larynx.

- **Trachea** – this is commonly known as the windpipe and is made up of rings of cartilage.

- **Bronchus** – this is at the base of the trachea and it branches out into the two smaller tubes known as the left and right bronchus.

- **Bronchioles** – the bronchi branch out into these smaller tubes.

- **Alveoli** – these are the air sacs where the bronchioles sub-divide. If spread out, they would cover over 55 square metres and there are literally millions of them. It is here that the exchange of oxygen and carbon dioxide takes place.

QUESTION SPOTTER

Some questions are as simple as just being able to name up to three of the air passages.

🏸 The lungs

- The lungs are the main organs for breathing and are protected inside the chest cavity by the ribs (at the back side and front) and the diaphragm (at the bottom). They have a very large surface area but the right lung is slightly larger than the left one as it has three sections (known as lobes), while the left one has only two.

- The lungs are surrounded by a layer of membrane known as the pleura which acts as a kind of lubricant. The majority of the lung is made up of alveoli and it is here that the process of gaseous exchange takes place.

QUESTION SPOTTER

It is very common to get a question asking what gaseous exchange is and exactly where it takes place.

🏸 Gaseous exchange

Gaseous exchange is the process that allows oxygen to be taken from the air and to be exchanged for carbon dioxide.

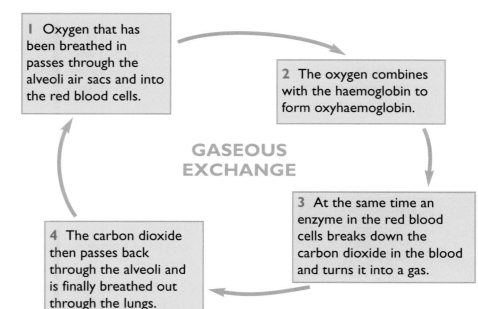

1 Oxygen that has been breathed in passes through the alveoli air sacs and into the red blood cells.

2 The oxygen combines with the haemoglobin to form oxyhaemoglobin.

GASEOUS EXCHANGE

3 At the same time an enzyme in the red blood cells breaks down the carbon dioxide in the blood and turns it into a gas.

4 The carbon dioxide then passes back through the alveoli and is finally breathed out through the lungs.

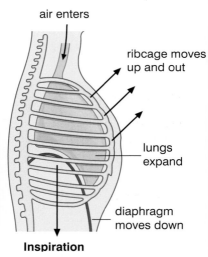

air enters

ribcage moves up and out

lungs expand

diaphragm moves down

Inspiration

🏸 The mechanism of breathing

- Breathing involves two movements:

  1 **Inspiration (breathing in)** – the ribs lift upwards and outwards, caused by the contraction of the intercostal muscles. At the same time, the diaphragm (a large muscle sheet that seals the chest cavity from the abdominal cavity) becomes flatter than its resting dome shape, and moves downwards. This makes the cavity larger, which reduces the pressure inside the chest cavity and causes air to be sucked into the lungs.

  2 **Expiration (breathing out)** – the reverse process takes place as the diaphragm relaxes at the same time as the intercostal muscles. The chest cavity returns to its normal size and the pressure on the lungs is increased, which forces the air out.

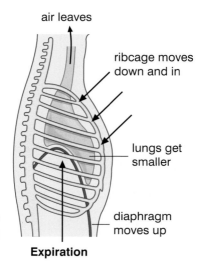

air leaves

ribcage moves down and in

lungs get smaller

diaphragm moves up

Expiration

The effect of exercise and training on the respiratory system

■ Regular exercise and training can benefit this system in the following ways:

• **Increased vital capacity** – this is the total volume of air that you can move in and out of the lungs in one deep breath. If this is increased, then a performer has an increased oxygen supply, which will allow the muscles to work harder and/or longer. As there is also an increased level of carbon dioxide being expelled, this also delays the build up of lactic acid (a poison that is a by-product of exercise and that causes fatigue) in the muscles.

• **Increased tidal volume** – this is the amount of air you breathe in and out normally with a normal breathing cycle. Increasing this means that you are able to deliver more oxygen and remove carbon dioxide quicker.

• **Increased oxygen debt tolerance** – this is the volume of oxygen consumed during recovery from exercise in excess of that which would normally be consumed in the same period. If a performer can maintain their performance for longer, this is a clear advantage – especially for performers in endurance-type events.

QUESTION SPOTTER

Being able to tell the difference between aerobic and anaerobic respiration is crucial as this is a very common question. You might be asked to give the equations for both aerobic and anaerobic respiration.

Skiing is an endurance event that is aerobic.

Aerobic and anaerobic respiration

■ **Aerobic respiration** is respiration that uses oxygen. It is summarised by the equation:

Glucose + oxygen → energy + carbon dioxide + water

■ Aerobic respiration is used when you are continuing with an activity for a long period of time. The process needs oxygen in order to produce energy.

- **Anaerobic respiration** is respiration in the absence of oxygen. It is summarised by the equation:

  Glucose → energy + lactic acid

- Anaerobic respiration is used only in short bursts and for short periods, since the body cannot tolerate too much lactic acid. Anaerobic respiration can be maintained only for about 40 seconds as a maximum.

Sprinting is a speed event that is anaerobic.

CHECK YOURSELF QUESTIONS

Q1 Define the following:
  a gaseous exchange
  b aerobic respiration
  c anaerobic respiration

Q2 What is the correct name for the windpipe?

Q3 Where exactly does gaseous exchange occur?

Q4 Are both lungs exactly the same size?

Q5 What is the diaphragm?

Q6 Which type of respiration would be required by the following performers?
  a a power lifter
  b a cross-country runner
  c an outfield hockey player

Answers are on page 145.

The five main factors

■ There are five main factors you must take into account when taking part in any form of training session. Each one of them has a specific effect on the body.

  1 The particular kind of activity or exercise you use to build up or improve certain body parts or skills is specificity.

  2 Making your body work harder than normal in order to make it adapt to improve is overload.

  3 Increasing the overload gradually and safely is progression.

  4 The loss of positive effects if you stop training is reversibility.

  5 Making sure that you train to be ready for a particular event or activity is peaking.

Specificity

■ Specificity within a training programme will vary for the following reasons:

  ● The type of person who is training – their initial fitness levels, body type and other physiological factors.

  ● The type of activity being trained for – the sport itself and the level at which it is to be performed.

Overload

■ Overload is usually linked to the acronym FITT (or FITT principle). This stands for:

  ● **F** – frequency, or how often it takes place

  ● **I** – intensity, or how hard you train

  ● **T** – the time, or duration, of each session

  ● **T** – type of training or exercise.

This weight-lifter is doing a bench press in order to increase upper body strength.

QUESTION SPOTTER

You will often be asked to define specificity and to explain why you need to consider it when planning a programme. Do not just repeat the word 'specific' – you need to define the term more precisely.

QUESTION SPOTTER

Questions about acronyms are very common. You may be given the letters FITT and be asked what they stand for. Sometimes you must give a brief explanation as well.

🏸 Progression

■ You must build progression into a training programme. You need to consider the following points fully:

- The levels of general and specific fitness that are in place at the start.

- You may have to start very gradually but you must increase the demands as your body adjusts to the work it is doing.

- A level of plateauing (getting to a certain level and then appearing to be stuck there before moving on) may happen. This can occur more than once.

Different people have different levels of fitness.

🏸 Reversibility

■ Reversibility will be felt if, for any reason, training either stops or is reduced.

- Positive effects will be lost at roughly the rate of one-third of the time it took to gain them!

- A beginner loses effects at a faster rate than a regular, trained performer.

- Different factors of fitness may be affected in different ways and to different degrees.

Sometimes reversibility may be forced through injury!

Peaking

- **Peaking** is essential to anyone who is taking part in some sort of competitive sport. This is because:

  - It is difficult to keep yourself fully fit at the highest level for a long time. There may be a competition, or event, that you are aiming to be at your best for.

  - Many activities have seasons, which are the times of the year an activity is played competitively. You would aim to be at your best during this playing season.

CHECK YOURSELF QUESTIONS

Q1 How would you define the following terms relating to the principles of training?
  a specificity
  b overload
  c progression
  d reversibility
  e peaking

Q2 Why are these five principles important when planning, and carrying out, any form of training?

Q3 What is the difference between overload and progression?

Q4 What are some of the safety factors you would have to consider when you are taking part in any form of training programme? Make these specific to a particular programme.

Q5 Consider an international standard sprinter. Why must they be able to peak in order to be successful?

Answers are on page 145.

■ Planning either a PEP (Personal Exercise Plan) or Health-related Exercise Training Programme will be one of the tasks you will have to complete as part of your practical coursework – it may also be a topic you will be examined on.

■ In order to plan a programme you need to be aware of the principles of training and also the factors of fitness (see Unit 4) in order to be able put your own programme together. Once you start to consider your PEP you will need to plan particular sessions. Within each session you will need to have particular phases.

Training session phases

■ All training sessions have particular phases that should be included. These are:

- warm-up
- fitness or exercise
- skill or team play
- warm-down – also known as cool-down.

The warm-up phase

■ The warm-up is essential in any training session (just as it is important before taking part in any form of exercise or activity):

- It prepares the body for the activity, raising the heart rate and breathing rate and stimulating the nervous system so you are psychologically prepared.
- It reduces the possibility of injury, notably muscle injury.

■ The warm-up should consist of:

- A continuous movement activity – often known as a pulse raiser.
- Light exercises – these would be targeted at certain muscle groups.
- Mobility exercises – stretches aimed at particular muscle groups and major joints.

■ The time spent on the warm-up phase, and the type of content included, will depend on:

- the type of activity being prepared for
- to some extent, the environment in which it is to be carried out.

The amount of time given to each training session phase.

QUESTION SPOTTER

Questions relating to warm-ups are extremely common. You must be able to give an example of a suitable and appropriate warm-up for at least one major game, so make sure you fully record a warm-up you have done or observed during practical sessions.

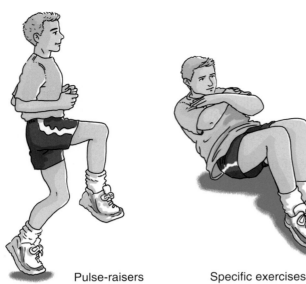

Pulse-raisers

Specific exercises

Stretching/mobility

Warm-up exercises.

Fitness or exercise phase

- The fitness or exercise phase will vary depending on what type of training session is being undertaken. For a general session (such as one for a PEP) this might consist of a selection of different exercises such as circuit training, or it might be specifically aimed at particular factors of fitness, such as strength, and carried out through weight training.

- It is important to consider the principles of specificity and overload in this particular phase in order to gain the full benefit.

Circuit training can be part of the fitness phase.

Skill or team play phase

- The skill phase may not be appropriate to all training sessions. For example, if it is just a general fitness session you may not aim to include specific skills within the session. However, it is advisable to introduce skills where appropriate as this is an additional opportunity to practise. Skill practice can help to avoid the tedium factor that can be part of a training session.

- Whether an activity is an individual or team one also becomes a factor here. This could provide an opportunity to develop some team skills. Once again, the principle of specificity is a crucial one in this phase.

Team activities, such as rugby, need lots of team skills.

Warm-down phase

- The warm-down is also an essential part of any training session and must be carried out for the following reasons:

  - To allow the body to return to its normal temperature.

  - To allow the pulse rate to return from its working level to its resting one.

  - To help prevent stiffness and soreness in the muscles by dispersing lactic acid.

- Warm-down activities can be similar to those included in the warm-up.

- An additional factor that should always be considered during training sessions is that of safety. You need to be aware of any safety aspects that apply to particular activities, training methods, equipment used and techniques (see Unit 11).

Warm-down activities, such as stretching exercises, allow the body to return to normal.

> ### QUESTION SPOTTER
>
> You may be asked why it is important to include a warm-down after exercising. (Be aware that the term 'cool-down' may be used – it means the same thing.)

? CHECK YOURSELF QUESTIONS

Q1 a Why are you be expected to include a warm-up in every training session you take part in?
b What type of warm-up activities would you include in a training session for either gymnastics or hockey?

Q2 How and why would you consider the principles of specificity and overload in a particular training session you organise? Give some examples.

Q3 When would it be appropriate to include a skill phase in a training session? Give an example from a relevant sport or activity.

Q4 Identify some particular safety considerations during a typical training session that would be specific to that particular session.

Answers are on page 146.

Planning, performing, monitoring and evaluating programmes

✏ Planning

- There are some general points regarding planning:

  - Are the goals you have set yourself realistic? The programme needs to be challenging but it also needs to be one that you are capable of following.

  - Can you predict some likely outcomes? Set these as targets so that you know why you are following the programme and what you may achieve at the end.

  - Consider all the options. There are various methods you can choose and it is wise to consider them all before settling on your final choice:

circuit training   weight training   interval training

choices for training method

fartlek training   continuous training

- Within your planning, you should include the following:

  - Some testing of your prior fitness/performance levels. Include in this any possible injuries or health problems.

  - Safety aspects – you must make sure you are planning a safe programme in terms of the equipment you are using, any supervision that may be necessary and the physical demands you are making on yourself.

  - How appropriate the content you have chosen is and whether or not it is going to match what you want to achieve.

  - The application of the programme in relation to the theory you have learned so that you take note of specificity, progression, overload and reversibility.

✏ Performing

- The programme should be performed over a minimum of six weeks. Remember that there must be some recovery time between sessions.

- You need to take the following factors into account when you are performing your programme:

  - How well are you implementing the programme? Are you able to complete it with control and consistently?

- Are you managing to complete all aspects of the programme in a safe and controlled way? You might find that you are being observed by a teacher when you are undertaking the programme so this would be an important factor.

- Are your attitude and motivation good? Are you moving towards those targets you set yourself in your initial planning?

- Are the warm-ups and warm-downs that you have included in your sessions both effective and appropriate?

■ Remember that when you are performing your programme, you are able to amend it if any of the above factors demands it. If, for example, you realise that you are not completing something in a safe way, then you should change it.

You will probably be observed performing your programme to make sure it is being performed properly.

Monitoring

■ Monitoring means keeping some sort of record of what you are actually doing so that you can keep a check on your progress. You can do this in the following ways:

- Use tables to record your results. You could set up a spreadsheet that covers your sessions and add the information to this.

- Make brief notes and comments after each session so that you have a diary that covers everything you have done.

- Record your heart rate and recovery rate as a regular part of each session to see how they have been affected.

⟡ Evaluating

■ At the end of the programme, you will be expected to make a final evaluation that draws together all of the factors you included in your programme. To do this, you should:

- **Evaluate your planning.** Evaluate whether all the elements you included worked well. This could, for example, cover whether the exercises you put into a circuit training programme were in the right order or whether you were able to apply the principles of training accurately.

- **Evaluate your performance.** You should be able to say whether or not you were able to perform as you intended. You should evaluate how manageable it was and also whether or not you found it enjoyable and interesting.

- **Evaluate the monitoring.** Did it go according to plan? Is the information you have collected in your table of results what you expected?

- **Include a final overall evaluation of the programme.** This would reflect how successful it was and what the next step might be in terms of any future planning or progression to further programmes.

CHECK YOURSELF QUESTIONS

Q1 Why is it important to check prior levels of fitness or performance before starting on a programme?

Q2 Why is it important to consider the order of activities in a programme, particularly in circuit training?

Q3 When you are performing your programme, what should you include at the start and the end of each session?

Q4 Why is it important to try to make your programme both interesting and enjoyable?

Answers are on page 146.

UNIT 9: TRAINING METHODS

 ◼ Circuit training ◼

🎾 Why exercise?

◼ Circuit training is one of the most common forms of training. It is popular because it is flexible and versatile.

🎾 Advantages of circuit training

◼ There are many advantages to circuit training:

  • Equipment can be very basic, simply benches and mats. It is even possible to run some circuits without any equipment.

  • Various components of fitness can be worked on and targeted for improvement, such as strength, power, flexibility, endurance and agility.

  • A wide range of exercises and activities can be included – this reduces the boredom factor.

A typical circuit in use.

  • The training principle of overload can easily be used (see page 50).

  • The circuit can be tailored for each individual's need, taking into account various fitness levels and work levels.

  • Both aerobic and anaerobic activities can be included.

  • All group sizes can be catered for – this could range from an individual up to a group as big as 40!

QUESTION SPOTTER

You may be asked what the advantages are of choosing circuit training as a form of training over other methods.

🎾 Organising a circuit

◼ It is not particularly difficult to organise a circuit. To make sure that it is effective, however, there are certain factors that need to be considered:

  • The areas (they are technically called stations) must be clearly laid out and labelled, making it apparent which particular exercise or activity is to be performed.

  • All of the activities/exercises should be clearly demonstrated to make sure that the group taking part is sure of the correct technique – this is also an important safety factor to consider. Regular checks should then also be made when the circuit is under way to make sure that these correct techniques continue to be used.

- The activities performed must be varied so that similar exercises do not follow each other. If there are three abdominal exercises in total in the circuit then they must be spread out evenly so that they do not follow each other. This is to allow a reasonable amount of recovery time for muscles or muscle groups.

- A recovery period must be included between each exercise so that the session is not continuous and the performer has a brief period of recovery before moving on to the next one.

- The 'work times' and 'rest times' must be clearly stated.

Types of circuit

- Circuits can be placed in two categories:

  - **Fitness circuits** – these are specifically designed to work on particular, or even general, aspects of fitness. These would include a variety of exercises such as press-ups, sit-ups, squat thrusts and star jumps.

  - **Skills circuits** – these are specifically designed to improve particular skills used in an activity. In basketball, for example, the circuit would contain various stations for skills that are important for basketball players, such as continuous chest passes against a wall, dribbling in and out of cones and continuous free throw shooting.

Continuous dribbling at speed would be a typical basketball skills station.

Running a circuit

- Circuits can be run in one of two ways:

  - Timed circuit – when using this, the performer performs the activity for a set time at each station and then rests. The time could be anything from 10 seconds up to a minute and it can be varied.

  - Fixed load – when using this approach, there is a set amount of work for each activity, such as performing 15 press-ups at that particular station.

- It is possible to change or integrate these two approaches, and to set the number of laps of the circuit each performer completes. You would normally be expected to complete more than one circuit and possibly as many as three.

- When doing this, the timings, or loads, can be adjusted for each lap – you can even have a 'sprint lap' at the start, which would be a form of warm-up with each exercise performed very briefly.

CHECK YOURSELF QUESTIONS

Q1 Which particular training principle can be particularly easily applied to circuit training?

Q2 What do you need to consider when planning the order of activities in a circuit?

Q3 Give two reasons why all the exercises/activities need to be demonstrated beforehand.

Q4 Name the two different types of circuit and briefly describe the two different ways of running them.

Answers are on page 146.

Weight, interval, continuous and fartlek training

🏸 Weight training

■ Weight training is primarily designed to improve strength, but it can also assist with:

- improving muscle tone
- increasing muscular endurance
- increasing speed
- developing muscle size, or bulk
- assisting recovery after injury.

A wide range of specialist weight training machinery is available.

ORGANISING SESSIONS

■ There are two terms that are particularly relevant to weight training. You must be familiar with these when referring to weight training sessions:

- **Repetitions** – this is the number of times you move the weights when training. If you were performing barbell curls and moved the weight up and down once then it would equal one repetition.

- **Sets** – this is the number of times you do a particular weight activity, so each time you complete your repetitions of the barbell curls you have done one set.

■ The way in which you vary, or adjust, the number of sets and repetitions is the basis of any weight training session.

■ The general rule is that for exercise to improve muscle tone you should use fairly light weights but have a high number of repetitions for about three sets. For more specific strength improvement, which would include building up muscle bulk, you would choose heavier weights with a small number of repetitions and an increased number of sets.

Adjustable freestanding weights are an alternative to fixed equipment.

> 💡 **QUESTION SPOTTER**
>
> Questions about the difference between repetitions and sets are common. Remember that they can refer to other forms of training as well, not just with weights.

WEIGHT TRAINING METHODS

■ Weight training methods make use of the specific ways in which muscles contract (see Unit 6):

- **Isotonic** – this is when the muscle contracts and works over a range of movement. For example, it occurs during a bicep curl throughout the entire movement of the arm being straightened out and then bent back in again (the flexion and extension movement).

- **Isometric** – this is when the muscle contracts but stays in a fixed position so that it is held at a particular point. Using the example of the bicep curl, the movement could be held when it is at the mid-point with the arm at right angles.

SAFETY FACTORS

■ When you are using weight training machines, there is little chance of accident or injury if you are using them properly. However, it is essential to be shown exactly how to use each machine and to use it in the correct way.

■ If you are working with freestanding weights, then you should have a training partner. He or she can help you load and unload weights and also assist with some of the weight training movements such as raising and lowering the bar on a bench press.

Interval training

■ Interval training is a form of training that consists of periods of work followed by periods of rest. It commonly involves running.

■ There are many combinations that can be used and the following factors have to be considered:

- The work time duration – this could be the distance run, or the length of time of a run.

- The intensity of the work – this could be the speed at which the run occurs.

- Repetitions – this could be the number of work repetitions or even the rest ones.

- Recovery time duration – this would normally refer to time but it could also be a distance, e.g. a measured slow walk distance.

■ The most important factor to consider in interval training is that the amount of work performed must be offset against the amount of rest, or recovery, that is allowed.

The full range of movement of the bicep curl is an isotonic contraction.

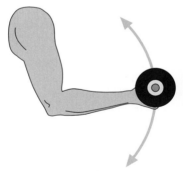

Stopping the movement at this point for several seconds is an isometric contraction.

ADVANTAGES OF INTERVAL TRAINING

- It requires virtually no equipment and can be performed anywhere.

- It can be very specific to activities or events – boxers often work for the same time a round of boxing would take, and have the same rest period between rounds.

- It is possible to raise the pulse rate to near maximal and work at a high training level.

- It is very well suited to anaerobic-type activities.

Marathon runners would use continuous training as their main training method.

Continuous training

- Continuous training is designed primarily to improve endurance as it keeps the heart and pulse rate high throughout an extended period. This can be achieved by running, jogging, cycling, swimming or even by taking part in an organised exercise session.

- The intention is to make sure that your body's demand for oxygen is matched by its oxygen uptake. In this way your aerobic fitness is targeted.

- This form of training meets any requirement as the beginner needs only to start with walking, either slowly or briskly. The more accomplished performer can work at higher levels of running.

QUESTION SPOTTER

It is common to be asked to state one or more of the forms of training. You may then be asked to outline the advantages of using a specific training form.

Fartlek training

- Fartlek is a Swedish word which means 'speed training', and it is a form of continuous training. It alternates walking, brisk walking, running, jogging and fast, steady running. It originated in the Scandinavian countryside, where it often involved running up hills.

- Many activities require levels of both aerobic and anaerobic activity. Fartlek training accommodates this with its constant change of pace.

? CHECK YOURSELF QUESTIONS

Q1 What is weight training primarily designed to improve?

Q2 What is meant by the following?
a repetitions
b sets

Q3 What is the difference between isotonic and isometric contractions?

Q4 What form of training alternates between periods of work and periods of rest?

Q5 What form of training would you recommend for the following types of performers?
a boxers
b soccer players
c marathon runners
d weight lifters
e sprinters

Answers are on pages 146–7.

UNIT 10: DRUGS AND SPORT

REVISION SESSION 1

Performance-enhancing drugs

■ Performance-enhancing drugs are drugs that performers take in order to improve their performance. Their use is banned by the ruling bodies of sport – performers caught using these drugs face a long ban from competing, plus large fines.

Prohibited drug classes

■ These have been identified by the governing bodies of sport.

STIMULANTS

■ **Stimulants** increase alertness, reduce fatigue and overcome tiredness. They may increase competitiveness and hostility. They include such substances as amphetamines, ephedrine, cocaine and even very high levels of coffee! Taking them regularly can produce unpleasant side effects such as high blood pressure, headaches, irregular heartbeat and addiction.

NARCOTIC ANALGESICS

■ **Narcotic analgesics** hide the effects of illness and injury and are a form of powerful painkiller. They include substances such as morphine, heroin, codeine and methadone. The side effects associated with them include loss of concentration, balance and co-ordination, exhaustion, dependence and apathy.

There have been at least two instances of cyclists dying while racing because they had taken stimulants.

ANABOLIC STEROIDS

- **Anabolic steroids** are the best known and most commonly abused drugs in sport. There are over one hundred different types of these drugs and more are being developed.

- These drugs are taken either as tablets or by injection. They increase muscle mass, which increases strength, so performers can train harder. They are commonly known as 'training drugs' because of this.

Sprinter Ben Johnson is an example of a performer guilty of taking anabolic steroids.

QUESTION SPOTTER

Questions about drug taking in sport tend to centre around anabolic steroids because they are the most common examples.

- The side effects are often linked to the fact that the drugs mimic the male hormone testosterone. Testosterone and anabolic steroids cause a deepening of the voice and the growth of facial hair. Other side effects include: liver and heart disorders, mood swings and aggression, reduced sperm production and infertility – in extreme cases they can even cause death.

DIURETICS

- **Diuretics** are used to increase the amount of urine produced, to increase kidney function and to expel water from the body at an accelerated rate. They cause rapid weight loss and are therefore often used by competitors in events that have weight categories. They are also sometimes used as 'masking agents' – to conceal other substances in the body.

- Side effects of these substances include dehydration, muscle cramps, headaches and nausea.

PEPTIDE AND GLYCOPROTEIN HORMONES

- **Peptide and glycoprotein hormones** produce effects similar to anabolic steroids since they artificially increase levels of hormones already in the body. Human growth hormone (HGH) is one of the most common, as is erythropoietin (EPO), which can artificially increase the aerobic capacity.

- Side effects include a high risk of heart attack or stroke since these hormones can thicken the blood. It therefore becomes more difficult for blood to pass through the small capillaries.

BETA-BLOCKERS

■ **Beta-blockers** have the effect of calming and controlling the heart and are prescribed to people who have heart conditions. They are an advantage to performers who need to have steady hands and remain relaxed, so there are many sports and events that ban their use.

BLOOD DOPING

■ **Blood doping** is not a banned substance but a banned procedure. It involves having a transfusion of blood. Blood is taken away and the performer trains with depleted blood levels. The blood is then replaced so that the body's red blood cell count is increased by up to 20% above its normal level. This has the overall effect of increasing the blood's oxygen-carrying capacity and would be a clear advantage to any performer in an endurance event.

Taking beta-blockers to steady your aim would give you an unfair advantage in shooting events.

? CHECK YOURSELF QUESTIONS

Q1 What are performance-enhancing drugs and why is their use banned in sport?

Q2 What is the main reason for a performer taking stimulants?

Q3 Which banned substance is also known as a 'training drug'?

Q4 For each of the following substances, name two sports or activities for each where taking them might be an advantage:
a diuretics
b beta-blockers

Q5 In what types of events would performers be tempted to make use of blood doping and why?

Answers are on page 147.

Social drugs

■ A drug is a chemical substance that, when introduced to the body, can alter the biochemical structure. Drugs fall into two categories:

- socially acceptable drugs;
- socially unacceptable drugs.

Socially acceptable drugs

■ Many people take drugs on a regular basis. These may be drugs that can be bought 'over the counter', such as paracetamol, or prescribed drugs that have to be taken for disorders such as asthma.

Not everyone realises that caffeine is a drug and in high doses is considered to be a stimulant.

Other drugs include:

- **Caffeine** – present in many fizzy drinks, coffee and tea.

- **Nicotine** – this is present in cigarettes. It can become addictive, which is why many people find it impossible to give up smoking.

- **Alcohol** – this can also be addictive and although it is not banned, there are instances when excess amounts in the bloodstream can be illegal, such as driving a car. Alcohol consumption is banned in events such as shooting, archery and fencing because small amounts can reduce stress and have a calming influence. In larger quantities, it would impair performance in the majority of events because it slows down reaction times and causes unsteadiness.

■ See Unit 1, page 2, for more detail on the harmful effects of smoking and alcohol.

Socially unacceptable drugs

■ A law was introduced in 1971 that identified a list of dangerous or harmful substances and called them 'controlled drugs'. This has effectively made them illegal and they fall into three categories:

- **Class A** – this includes opium, heroin methadone, hallucinogens, amphetamines and designer drugs such as 'Ecstasy'.

- **Class B** – this includes stimulant amphetamines.

- **Class C** – other amphetamines, tranquillisers and sedatives. Cannabis and cannabis resin are now classified as class C drugs, although before January 2004 they were classified as class B.

■ Using the drugs listed above can result in prosecution but there are also penalties for any sports performers caught using them. There are many examples where individuals have been caught and banned from their sport.

✎ Drug use in sport

■ The first recorded case of drug taking in sport was in 1865 and there have been many cases since then in all sports and sporting events. Because of this, regular drug testing is present in all sports and at all major sporting events. The first time drug tests were used in an Olympic Games was in 1968 at the Summer and Winter Olympics.

■ In the majority of cases, the performers are caught using performance-enhancing drugs to improve their performance, but many are also caught using social or 'recreative drugs' which have become part of their lifestyle.

■ Sprinters Ben Johnson and Dwain Chambers both failed drug tests and were banned from taking part in their sport.

■ One of the major problems for the drug testers is that new drugs are being developed. This means that new tests that can identify them must be developed.

QUESTION SPOTTER

As there are so many instances of drug-taking in sport you might well be asked to give a recent example.

? CHECK YOURSELF QUESTIONS

Q1 What is the difference between a socially acceptable drug and a socially unacceptable drug?

Q2 Give an example where taking a small amount of alcohol could be seen to be an advantage to a performer.

Q3 What does a drug do? Are all drugs harmful?

Answers are on page 147.

REVISION SESSION 1

General rules

■ All performers have to be aware of the potential hazards of taking part in any form of physical activity. There are many general rules you need to be aware of, and general precautions you can take.

🎾 Environment/playing area

■ The actual environment could include the following factors:

- **The weather** may be extremely cold or very hot! If the temperature is very low, then outdoor areas may be frozen and unplayable. If it is very high, then the ground may be too hard for certain activities and the high temperatures could result in sunburn and dehydration. It is not possible to play certain sports if there are thunderstorms – golf tournaments have play suspended during such storms.

- **Playing areas** need to be very carefully checked to make sure that they are safe. Outdoor areas could have dangerous objects such as glass, stones, damaged fencing or protruding post sockets. These may result in serious cuts, abrasions or even fractures. Indoor areas may have slippery floors, or equipment that has not been stored away properly.

🎾 Equipment

■ This includes the following categories:

- **Playing equipment** – always use the correct equipment for the activity being performed. Safety helmets would be appropriate for cricket but not for rugby! Equipment must also be worn correctly, with laces done up and any loose straps tucked away. Checks must also be made to ensure that equipment is in good condition – splinters from damaged hockey sticks or rounders bats can be dangerous. Large pieces of equipment such as soccer, hockey and rugby posts must be checked to make sure they are safe.

- **Footwear/clothing** – many sports have their own specific protective clothing. This includes such things as shin-guards, gum shields and strap-on pads. Some activities have rules that ensure that this equipment is used and worn.

  Footwear needs to be correct and appropriate. Certain surfaces require particular footwear to be worn. For example, special trainers with soles that grip well have been developed for use on Astroturf.

> ### 💡 QUESTION SPOTTER
>
> You may be asked to identify potential hazards and to describe how they could contribute to particular injuries.

This field hockey goalie wears protective equipment to cover every vulnerable spot.

Prior preparation

- Getting ready before taking part includes the following:

  - **Training** to the correct level to be able to take part – you would not take part in a marathon without training hard beforehand.

  - **Warming-up** – this should always be part of your initial preparation.

  - **Physical state** – this includes removing all items of jewellery, even making sure that fingernails are short (there is a specific rule in netball regarding this) and putting on the correct clothing and equipment.

  - **Learning the rules** of the activity – you could be a danger to yourself and others if you went into a hockey match or rugby game with no knowledge of the rules.

Participation

- When you are taking part you need to consider the following:

  - **Fair play** – you must play by the rules. A high tackle in rugby is illegal because it is extremely dangerous. Rules aim to eliminate all forms of foul play.

  - **Obeying officials** – the official in charge of an activity often gives instructions that must be obeyed. This is especially relevant to any contact sports.

  - **Balanced competition** – nearly all sports insist that activities are played in age groups to make sure that competition is fair and safe. Some others also insist that there are weight categories – this is especially true for combat sports and martial arts. It is also a general rule that only single sex competition is allowed in many major games, especially those involving any form of physical contact.

Both sexes can participate where there is no physical contact.

? CHECK YOURSELF QUESTIONS

Q1 What are the potential hazards of taking part in an outdoor event if the weather is extremely cold?

Q2 Why would an official carefully check a hockey, rugby or soccer pitch before a game got underway?

Q3 What specific footwear would a hockey player need to be wearing to play a match on a grass pitch?

Q4 Why should all jewellery be removed before taking part in sport?

Q5 Which sport has a particular rule regarding the length of fingernails?

Answers are on page 147.

REVISION SESSION 2

Activity-specific safety and risk assessment

■ As well as the general rules, you also need to know the more specific ones that apply to each of the National Curriculum activity areas.

Games activities

■ There are three types of games:

- **Invasion games** – nearly all of these games require specialist equipment if they are to be played safely. Several also allow physical contact so it would not be permissible for them to be performed in mixed sex groups. The standard safety equipment appropriate for these activities includes gum shields, shin pads and goalkeeping gloves. Examples of invasion games are hockey and basketball.

- **Net/wall games** – these are usually played indoors, so the main consideration is that the immediate playing area is safe and that the right footwear is worn. Another safety consideration is that any rackets used are in good condition and are not likely to snap or break. Examples of these games are badminton and tennis.

- **Striking/hitting games** – as these involve a ball being struck, there may be requirements for certain players to wear particular safety equipment. Players may also have to be appropriate distances away from the batter. Playing areas are normally outside so they must be safe – it is not possible to play rounders safely on wet grass. Examples of these games are rounders and cricket.

Trampoline sessions must be led by a qualified person and there must be spotters around the trampoline.

Gymnastic activities

■ The equipment used must be safe: this ranges from agility mats, to vaulting boxes and even to trampolines as trampolining is classed as a gymnastic activity. Such equipment must be moved and erected safely.

■ A qualified person must be in charge of gymnastic activities – including trampolining.

Dance activities

- Dance is not generally considered to be a high-risk activity. However, performers must make sure that any mats used are in good condition, without gaps between them where toes could be trapped.

- Jewellery must be removed and a full warm-up must be included. The correct clothing must be worn. Specialist dance areas often have sprung floors to allow better movement. These floors have to be checked for damage.

Athletic activities

- Athletic activities can be divided into three areas:

  1 **Throwing events** – the throwing area and the item being used must be considered. Javelins are clearly very dangerous, but people have been killed by being struck by a discus, so precautions must be taken. Nobody should be in front of the thrower at any time and the time of the throw must be carefully controlled. The handling, carrying and placing of the equipment must also be done safely.

  2 **Jumping events** – the immediate area must be checked; sandpits need to be checked for any dangerous or sharp objects. Rakes must be carefully held and landing mats must be checked for damage and wear and tear.

  3 **Track events** – the running area must be checked and the correct footwear must be worn, such as spikes for additional grip.

A javelin is clearly a potentially dangerous object to throw.

Swimming activities

- All pools have a large number of safety regulations and rules. Swimming should take place only under qualified supervision, with a lifeguard in the area.

- Specific rules, such as not running around the pool area, checking the depth of water and not diving or jumping in certain areas, are all important. If the swimming is taking place outdoors in the sea or a lake, there is even greater need for careful safety measures and qualified supervision.

All swimming sessions should be supervised by a qualified lifeguard.

Outdoor and adventure
activities

- Adventure activities are potentially the
  most dangerous of all activities and the
  ones where there is the highest chance
  of serious injury. A lot of planning and
  preparation are necessary.

- The environment is clearly crucial because
  activities such as abseiling, canoeing and
  climbing take place in potentially dangerous
  areas. Weather conditions – and weather
  forecasts – must be considered carefully for
  activities such as walking, mountaineering
  and even potholing.

- Correct equipment is vital and these activities
  must be led by a fully qualified instructor.

*Some activities are clearly
potentially dangerous.*

? CHECK YOURSELF QUESTIONS

Q1 What types of activity cannot be played
by mixed sex groups?

Q2 If a grass playing area is wet, which
activities could not be played?

Q3 What specific equipment would a hockey
goalkeeper need to wear?

Q4 What would be the main safety
consideration for any swimming or
water-based activity?

Q5 Why might a change in the weather be
dangerous if you were potholing?

Answers are on pages 147–8.

UNIT 12: INJURIES

REVISION SESSION 1 — Types and treatment of injuries

■ You need to be able to identify particular injuries and learn about appropriate treatments for them.

Joint injuries

■ Joint injuries occur in and around joints. The most common are:

- **Strain** – this is an injury to a muscle or a tendon, usually caused by overstretching, although it can also be caused by a twist or a wrench. The area can be bandaged and the RICE treatment (see page 79) can be used.

- **Sprain** – this is an injury to a ligament at a joint, usually caused by overstretching or tearing. Sprains are also caused by a twist or wrench and are very common in the ankle. The RICE treatment is again appropriate.

- **Dislocation** – this occurs only at joints and is where one bone comes out of its normal position against another. It is usually caused by a hard blow to the area. The main sign that dislocation has occurred is that the joint appears deformed and the person will not be able to move it. This injury must be dealt with by an expert: on no account should anyone try to put the joint back into place.

QUESTION SPOTTER

An *extremely* popular question is what the difference is between a strain and a sprain. Remember that a strain is an injury to a muscle or tendon and a sprain is an injury to a ligament at a joint.

Fractures

■ A fracture is a break or crack in a bone. There are three main types of fractures:

- **Simple, or closed** – this is where a bone is broken but it does not pierce the skin.

- **Compound, or open** – this is where the skin is broken so the bone can be seen sticking out through a wound.

- **Complicated** – this is where there is serious damage to a nerve or blood vessel, which can cause bleeding.

■ You may well hear the sound of a snap when a bone fractures. There will be a lot of pain, and it will probably not be possible to move the part of the body around the break.

■ The main treatment is to support the area and, if possible, to apply a splint so the damaged bone is kept straight. This injury needs expert help quickly, so call an ambulance.

 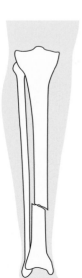 

simple fracture   compound fracture   complicated fracture

✎ Skin damage

- Skin injuries fall into the following categories:

  - **Cuts** – these are open wounds, which allow blood to escape from the body. They should be gently cleaned and dressed. A plaster will be enough for small cuts but larger ones may require a bandage. Severe cuts require hospital treatment since it may be necessary to stitch the wound to stop the bleeding.

  - **Bruises** – this is where the blood vessels have been damaged but the skin has not been broken, so the bleeding occurs beneath the skin. There will be swelling in the area plus discoloration of the skin. Applying ice is the best treatment as this reduces the swelling and lessens the pain.

  - **Blisters** – these are extremely common and are caused by friction on the skin, which causes a break in the layers of the skin. The small gap between the layers fills up with a liquid called serum and the blister forms in a bubble shape. Blisters should be left to disperse on their own. For comfort they may be covered with plasters to reduce any rubbing.

✎ Concussion

- This is an injury to the brain which may be caused by a blow to the head. It can result in someone becoming unconscious. In this case, you should take the following action, using the DRABC mnemonic:

  - **Danger**, both to the injured person and the rescuer. Assess the situation, and fetch help if necessary. For example, do not climb down to someone who has fallen if the climb is difficult.

  - **Response**, which means to check for any movement or speech and send for help immediately if there is no response.

  - **Airway** – check that the injured person's airway is clear so they can breathe.

This is the recovery position, with the hand supporting the head and the head tilted back to keep the airways open.

  - **Breathing** – listen at the mouth and feel the chest to see if it rises.

  - **Check** the pulse.

- If there are signs of breathing, place the person in the recovery position.

⚃ Dehydration

■ Dehydration was covered in Unit 2 (page 9). It is caused by a rapid loss of water from the body and can result in nausea, extreme tiredness and even dizziness. It is important to prevent this situation, so take fluids regularly.

⚃ Hypothermia

■ Hypothermia is rapid cooling of the body when the body temperature falls below 35 °C. At this temperature, the pulse rate tends to slow, the person shivers and the skin goes cold and pale. It is important to make sure that any wet clothing is removed and that the person is re-warmed gradually by raising their core body temperature.

⚃ Winding

■ Winding is caused by a blow to the abdominal area, which temporarily paralyses the diaphragm muscle and causes great difficulty in breathing. The person should be placed in a seated position or encouraged to bend up and down at the waist in order to get air back into the lungs.

⚃ Cramp

■ Cramp is an involuntary contraction of a muscle and, although quite painful, it is easy to relieve. You have to stretch the muscle as far as it will go. Cramp often occurs in the calf muscle and to relieve it, you can straighten the knee and bend the foot back upwards at the ankle.

This is how to relieve cramp in the calf muscle.

❓ CHECK YOURSELF QUESTIONS

Q1 **a** Which injury is caused by overstretching a muscle or a tendon?

   b Which injury is caused by overstretching a ligament at a joint?

Q2 Name the three different types of fracture.

Q3 What is the basic treatment to give a fracture?

Q4 What should you apply to a bruise to help the swelling go down?

Q5 What is the difference between hypothermia and dehydration?

Answers are on page 148.

Basic first aid

✎ General rules for treatment

- These general rules apply in all situations – more specific treatment may be required for particular injuries:

  - Do not move anyone who has an injury until you are sure what the problem is.
    If in any doubt, you should phone for an ambulance.

  - Look for cuts, wounds or misshapen joints. See if the person can move the affected area – never try to move it for them!

  - If they are able to move, see if they can sit and then stand and bear their own weight.

  - If they are not able to go through these gradual stages, then you must get expert help immediately.

Do not move any injured person until you are sure the injury is not serious.

✎ Soft tissue injury treatment

- Soft tissue injury treatment is needed when there is any injury to ligaments or muscles. It includes sprains, strains and tears and slight muscle pulls.

- The treatment that should be given is the RICE treatment.

- RICE treatment stands for the following:

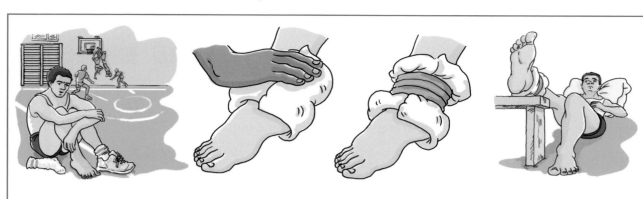

- **Rest** – stop immediately; the player must not carry on playing.

- **Ice** – apply ice immediately to the injured area. Make sure you do not apply the ice directly to the area. It must be wrapped in something or it can cause skin damage.

- **Compression** – with either a bandage or a tape, use pressure to keep the ice pack in position. This will reduce bleeding and swelling.

- **Elevation** – raise the injured part above the level of the heart, as this decreases the circulation and helps drain away any fluid at the injury point.

Slings and bandages

- If slings and bandages are available, and you know how to apply them correctly, then they can be used to support injured limbs or placed over wounds.

Sprays and medications

- Sprays and medications should never be used by anyone not specifically trained to use them. Even if they are available in first aid kits, you should not be tempted to use them as there is a chance that you will do more harm than good.

- Remember that you should not attempt any significant treatment and you should not presume exactly what an injury is. The symptoms of a strain, sprain and fracture are almost identical and a hospital X-ray is usually necessary for correct diagnosis. If there is any doubt at all, you must call expert help, which will often involve telephoning for an ambulance.

QUESTION SPOTTER

It is very common to get a question asking you what is meant by the RICE principle. You need to be able to state what each letter stands for.

CHECK YOURSELF QUESTIONS

Q1 What is the basic rule about moving anyone who has received an injury?

Q2 What should you do in any circumstance if you are not sure of the extent of an injury?

Q3 What do the letters RICE stand for?

Q4 For what sort of injury might you apply a sling?

Answers are on page 148.

UNIT 13: SKILL ACQUISITION

How skills are learned

- **Skill** is the ability to use knowledge or expertise to succeed efficiently and effectively in achieving a particular objective.

- In PE, this definition means you should be able to perform physical activities with a high degree of control, consistency and accuracy. These are the main factors that your performance will be judged against in the practical component of your GCSE exam.

Levels of skill

- Different skills are used by performers at different levels of sport – from the novice, or beginner, up to the expert, or even professional.

  - **Basic skills** – these are the simpler things such as moving, running, jumping and catching. Simply controlling your body movement is a basic skill. There may be some movements, such as sprinting, dodging and weaving, that are needed in several activities.

  - **Complex skills** – these are more advanced skills that take quite a long time to learn as they require a high level of co-ordination and control. An activity such as the pole-vault is a good example of a complex skill as it requires a high degree of very skilled, co-ordinated movement.

Learning and developing skills

- Some skills, such as catching, can be learnt in one go and this is known as 'whole learning'. More difficult skills have to be broken down into particular parts and are known as 'part learning'. A tennis serve is a good example of this as you have to break down the various parts of the action and contact with the ball.

  - **Practice** is essential if you are to acquire skill. A performer must be prepared to spend a considerable amount of time practising the whole skill and parts of it.

  - **Demonstration and copying** – most skills are learnt through watching the correct way to perform them. Teachers, trainers and coaches will often demonstrate particular skills to show how they should be performed.

> **QUESTION SPOTTER**
>
> It is common to be asked to explain the difference between a basic and complex skill.

Diving involves a great deal of complex skill.

To learn how to serve at tennis requires part skill learning.

• **Trial and error** – each performer has to try out skills and practise them. Initially they may not get them right, so they have to work on them over a period of time.

Information processing

■ We are able to use information stored in our memories to improve our performance. This works in the following way:

• **Input** – this is what is going on around you as you perform. It could be the people around you or the flight of a ball.

• **Decision making** – using the input, you then have to make a decision about what you are going to do, e.g. whether to pass to the person near to you or keep the ball yourself.

• **Output** – this is the result of the input and decision making because it is what actually happens.

• **Feedback** – this is the information you get back at the end of the process. It is dealt with in more detail in the next revision session (page 83).

Applying skills

■ Once you have learnt skills, you then have to apply them properly. This is what often singles out top players – they are able to select the correct skill at the right time. Cricketers who choose to play the wrong shot to a particular type of delivery will find themselves getting out, not through lack of skill but through poor application.

■ Many skills are transferable from one sport to another. For instance, the throwing and fielding skills at rounders are about the same as for cricket and would be easily transferable.

Many skills can be transferred between striking/hitting games such as cricket and rounders/softball.

⚡ Types of skill

■ These fall into two categories:

- **Open skills** – these are skills that are used in constantly changing situations. Changing conditions include the weather (wind is particularly important), team-mates and opponents. There is a need to constantly change or adapt skills according to these factors.

- **Closed skills** – these are skills that occur in an environment that is constant and not changing. Trampolinists perform on a piece of apparatus that is constant. They are able to perform the same skills again and again without anything external changing.

■ Remember that not all skills fit neatly into these two categories – many activities have phases where there are both open and closed skill situations. For example, a pole vaulter would use open skills for the approach, but the final phase, involving the rotation over the bar, would be a closed skill.

This trampolinist is performing a closed skill.

CHECK YOURSELF QUESTIONS

Q1 What two different levels of skills exist for performers?

Q2 What is the difference between 'whole' learning and 'part' learning?

Q3 Why would a coach or teacher choose to demonstrate a particular skill to a pupil?

Q4 What are the four factors that have to be considered for information processing?

Q5 What is meant by the term 'transfer of skill'?

Q6 Describe an activity where there are both open and closed skill situations.

Answers are on page 148.

Feedback to improve skills

🎾 Definition

■ The information you receive during and after your performance is known as feedback. There are several types:

- **Intrinsic feedback** – is sensed, or felt, by the performer while they are performing. Beginners may not be able to make a great deal of use of this, as they lack experience. More experienced performers will be able to tell for themselves where they are going wrong and take steps to correct it.

- **Extrinsic feedback** – comes from sources other than the performer. This could be sounds from the crowd, things the performer can see or hear during the performance or a debriefing from a teacher or coach after the performance. Feedback can be very formally given, such as a half-time talk from the coach or captain, or it can just be shouted comments as a game progresses.

- **Knowledge of performance** – is how well a performance was done rather than just the end result. The performance needs to be analysed, which is why it is now very common to video a performance. The video is watched by the performer later when the teacher or coach may make comments about the performance.

- **Knowledge of results** – is the information you receive at the end of a performance. It is sometimes known as terminal feedback. It could be as basic as whether you won or lost, your finishing position or the distance you managed on a throw.

QUESTION SPOTTER

You may be asked to identify the various forms of feedback, or you may be asked about one of them in particular.

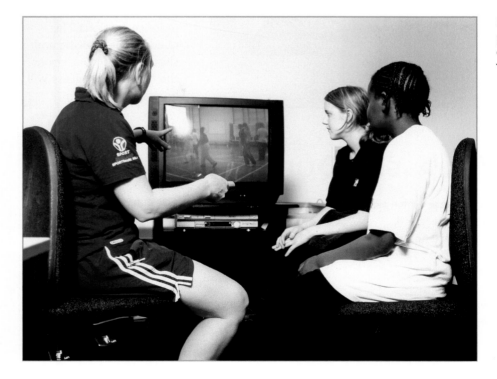

Being able to watch your performance on video is one of the most effective forms of feedback.

⚡ Types of guidance

■ A teacher gives most of the guidance in school. However, there may be occasions when pupils are expected to give each other advice and guidance. You need to consider the following:

- **What to feed back on?** Too much information can be difficult to take in, so it is better to focus on particular aspects of a performance. The feedback therefore needs to be selective. If it was a team game, you would also have to decide who you were going to feedback to – individuals or the whole team.

- **When to feed back?** The best time is usually just after the performance while it is still fresh in the memory. However, it can also often be continuous and given to the performer as the performance is developing.

Team talks are a very common way of giving feedback and guidance.

- **How often to feed back?** It should be regular if it is to have any impact. You should try to make it positive rather than too negative. It should certainly be done after each performance.

- **Goal setting.** This should be part of the feedback. It will identify specific aspects of the performance that can be targeted for improvement and included in future practice sessions. This needs to be realistic and should take into account the fact that progress will be gradual.

❓ CHECK YOURSELF QUESTIONS

Q1 For each of the following, state which type of feedback would be being received.

    a A gymnast realising they are not holding their balances with enough body tension

    b A crowd calling to a player that an opponent is about to tackle them

    c A sprinter being awarded a gold medal at the end of a competition

    d You watching a video replay of your own performance

Q2 When would be the best time to feed back to a performer who has taken part in a training session?

Q3 What does goal setting mean?

Answers are on page 148.

UNIT 14: TECHNOLOGY

REVISION SESSION I

Equipment, clothing and facilities

✎ Equipment

- There have been considerable developments in equipment for all sports in recent years. This has mainly been due to the use of new materials. Examples include the following:

  - **Racket sports.** Rackets used for tennis, badminton and squash used to be wooden framed but they have evolved through aluminium to, most recently, graphite. The rackets are now much lighter and stronger and players can therefore generate more power. The size and shape of rackets have also changed. This has also resulted in increased power – although players have to balance power with control.

  - **Athletics.** Various events have evolved as equipment has become available. The 'Fosbury flop' high-jump technique can be used only with the correct landing area equipment in place – it could not be performed in a conventional sandpit! Pole-vaulters now jump over greater heights because of the fibreglass compound used in their poles, which replaced metal and, before that, wood. The centre of gravity of javelins had to be changed because they were being thrown so far the stadiums were not large enough to cope with the distances.

> • For AQA Specification A candidates only.

> This jumping technique is possible only because of developments in landing equipment.

  - **Measuring and recording.** Equipment is now available to check if the ball is in or out in tennis, with the information being relayed to the umpire. Sprint races are timed to thousandths of seconds and there are even sensors in starting blocks to let the starter know if there is a false start! Sensors are used in marathon races to check if all runners cover all parts of the course. In fencing, sensors are inserted in suits to check whether hits are made or not.

> **💡 QUESTION SPOTTER**
>
> A common question is to ask for examples of ways in which technology has led to improvements in performance.

✒ Clothing

■ Clothing is constantly evolving, with new types of materials enabling performers to make minute, but significant, improvements to their performance.

Ian Thorpe pioneered the wearing of these all-in-one swimming suits to improve swim times.

- **Body suits.** These were first worn by speed skaters, then by sprinters and more recently by swimmers. The materials reduce the amount of drag or wind resistance and, in the case of the swimmers, allow them to move through the water slightly quicker.

- **Safety equipment.** This is now both lighter and stronger. Cricketers wear far more safety equipment than they used to because it does not slow them down unnecessarily, and it gives them added protection. The situation is similar for hockey goalkeepers who now have far lighter safety equipment.

- **Footwear.** This is now very specialised for all sports, with each sport having its own specifically designed, correct footwear. Marathon running shoes have air bubbles to reduce impact injuries; basketball boots have built-in ankle protectors; running shoes have specific surface spikes; Astroturf trainers provide correct grip; and soccer boots have various stud options for different surfaces.

✒ Facilities

■ Facilities now tend to be purpose-built, unlike older, general sports facilities such as hall and gyms. Some examples of changes include the following:

- **Gymnastics.** Facilities are now provided with sprung floors for tumbling and safety pits beneath the specialist gymnastic equipment – this is especially true of purpose-built training facilities. Previously, mats would have placed on the floor in a multi-use indoor area.

- **Stadiums.** These are now purpose-built and tend to have retractable roofs so that they are not affected by the weather. There are plans to put such a roof over the Centre Court at Wimbledon in the near future.

? CHECK YOURSELF QUESTIONS

Q1 Which materials have been introduced that have changed the design and effectiveness of rackets?

Q2 Why was it necessary to change the design of javelins?

Q3 Why were sensors introduced in tennis?

Q4 Why would a top-class swimmer be likely to wear an all-in-one body suit?

Q5 When a major sporting stadium is built, why is it now likely to have a retractable roof?

Answers are on page 148.

🏸 Use in sport

- The applied use of Information Communication Technology (ICT) is having an immense impact on sport. It is also constantly changing as technology evolves. The following are some of the examples where it is currently being used:

  - **Websites.** These are set up to provide all sorts of information to do with sport. Some provide information from the governing bodies of sports; others are interactive sites that show examples of sporting techniques and procedures, and training and testing examples.

  - **Computer programs.** Programs used in professional soccer and cricket can track and analyse the contribution and performance of particular members of the team. Television companies are testing programs that can make LBW (leg before wicket) decisions at cricket or line call decisions at tennis, using laser technology. The TV commentators would then use the computer's decisions as part of their commentary. Governing bodies are deciding whether to introduce such programs for their officials.

  - **DVDs and CD-ROMs.** These provide information or instruction on many topics and it is even possible to create virtual games for some sports.

  - **Video.** Video is used for slow motion and instant replay in many sports. Rugby now has the option of a video replay to see if a try has been scored and cricket has the 'third umpire' who rules on decisions through the use of playbacks.

  - **Communications.** Rugby referees are in contact with their touch judges and video officials through radio links. Soccer referees have sensors on their arms linked to transmitters in the assistant's flags to let them know when they are flagging for an offence.

> ### 💡 QUESTION SPOTTER
>
> You may well be asked how ICT can be used to make sport fairer and easier to judge.

Cricket's 'third umpire' uses ICT to help with difficult umpiring decisions. He replays the action on video and relays his decision to the umpire on the pitch.

Use in schools

QUESTION SPOTTER

Questions on this area of the theory often centre on the ways in which ICT can improve knowledge and also how it can improve performance.

The use of computers to access information is one of the most common forms of ICT in school.

■ ICT is increasingly being used in schools:

- **Spreadsheets** can be used by teachers and pupils to collect data together for interpretation.

- **Digital cameras** can be used to analyse and improve performances.

- **Visual analysis systems** that make use of video cameras and laptop computers enable pupils to make detailed analysis of their own, and others', performances. This is often a coursework requirement for pupils, who must be able to show how a performance could be improved. A visual analysis system can show performers details of their performance. This allows them to make judgements about how to improve it.

- **Multi-media devices** are used for dance, which allow light and sound to enhance the performance.

- **Training aids.** These vary from heart rate monitors, which can check the training zones you are working in, to blood pressure and breathing rate monitors. There are also accurate timing devices, which can be used to measure performance where time is an important factor.

- **Internet access.** Most schools now have ICT suites where pupils are able to access a great deal of information, especially about theory aspects of their course.

CHECK YOURSELF QUESTIONS

Q1 How might a sport such as soccer use video replays to make competition fairer?

Q2 Explain how schools can make use of video analysis systems.

Q3 In which types of activities would using accurate timing devices be a valuable ICT aid?

Answers are on page 149.

UNIT 15: OFFICIALS

The role of rules

■ All physical activities have rules that govern exactly how a game, or activity, should be played, or conducted. The reasons are:

- **To aid and assist in the organisation** – needing to know how many players make up a team, the rules for substitutes, pitch sizes and dimensions are just a few examples of this.

- **For efficient administration** – the rules that apply from the top to the bottom of each individual sport enable the governing bodies to run the sport more efficiently.

- **Safety** – without rules, all activities would be more dangerous because there would be no guidelines to ensure safe, fair play. This is the most important reason for rules.

- **Enjoyment** – all participants are able to take part on an equal basis, knowing exactly what the activity consists of. Without rules it is likely that there would be much less enjoyment.

> - All the specifications consider the role of rules and officials in the practical component.
> - AQA Specification A also covers the subject in the theory content, and it may be tested in the examination.

It is important that everyone involved is clear about the rules of the sport they are playing.

Rule enforcement

■ Rules must be enforced to be effective. Different sports have different ways in which they seek to enforce their rules. The following are the most common:

The use of the 'sin bin' in rugby is a form of temporary suspension.

- **Suspension** – this can be temporary within the game. Both ice hockey and rugby have 'sin bins' where offenders are sent to cool down. There are also more permanent suspensions when players are banned from playing a certain number of games.

- **Expulsion** – this is where the player, or competitor, is required to leave the game or is 'sent off', usually for a severe offence or repeated offences. All games have this measure and often the player is shown a red card by the official in charge. In basketball, you can be 'fouled out' after your allowed number of personal fouls have been committed.

- **Bans** – these are longer than suspensions. They are given for serious offences such as drug-taking (see Unit 10). Some performers may be banned from their sport permanently.

- **Fines** – these occur at all levels of sport, from amateur to professional. The only real difference is in the level of the fine – some professional performers can be fined thousands of pounds for breaking the rules.

Etiquette

■ Etiquette is not, strictly speaking, a rule but a conventional form of behaviour, or an unwritten rule. It reflects fair play and good sporting behaviour and is generally accepted as the correct way to participate. There are various examples of this in sports:

• **Cricket** – a batter should 'walk' when they know they are out. A new batter is welcomed to the crease by applause from the fielders.

Stopping play to allow a player to receive treatment is correct sporting etiquette.

• **Racket sports** – players call their own double hits and 'not up' shots that are almost impossible for the officials to correctly judge.

• **Soccer** – if a player is injured, the opponents kick the ball out of play to stop the game and allow the player to receive treatment. At the re-start, the ball is then returned to the team who played it out.

Rule changes

■ These are fairly common and occur for the following reasons:

• **Technology developments** – as technology improves equipment and materials (see Unit 14), the rules may have to be amended to cater for this, even to the point of banning some developments.

• **Safety** – this is one of the main reasons for changing a rule. It was only comparatively recently that the wearing of shin pads in soccer was made a rule. Rules have been introduced in junior cricket regarding the wearing of helmets.

• **Attraction and excitement** – these changes are made to make the activity more attractive to the spectator. The tie break rule was introduced in tennis to make it more exciting. The media (see Unit 18) are often instrumental in these rule changes.

> **QUESTION SPOTTER**
>
> It is common to be asked to describe what etiquette is and also to give a sporting example of when it occurs.

? CHECK YOURSELF QUESTIONS

Q1 What is the most important reason for having rules?

Q2 What are the two different types of suspensions that players might be given for breaking the rules?

Q3 What would being shown a 'red card' mean in team games?

Q4 What is meant by etiquette?

Q5 What role do the media play in rule changes?

Answers are on page 149.

REVISION SESSION 2 — Types of officials and their roles

■ As part of your GCSE coursework, you will be expected to adopt the role of an official, so it is important to know what this might involve. All activities have officials and they exist at all levels. In professional sport, they are now more likely to be full-time, paid officials.

Responsibilities

■ Officials organise and control the activity through interpreting the rules. They must make sure that the activity is being played safely. There are various types of officials:

- **Referees** – these are the most common and they are usually in charge of a game or match. The other common forms of senior officials are umpires and judges. These are the people who are in overall charge of an activity.

- **Assistant officials** – these are the more minor officials who assist in certain areas of the game but do not have overall control. They can include line judges, timekeepers, scorers or 'fourth officials' and video judges.

■ Most activities have a variety of officials in charge. In tennis, for example, a game played at a low level might just have an umpire in charge but at the top level there could be up to twelve officials allocated to each match.

QUESTION SPOTTER

You might be asked to state the difference between a minor and senior official and to give examples of each.

At the top level, badminton would require more than one umpire as the official in a competition.

✎ Qualities

■ To be an effective official, you must have certain qualities:

Football referees need to be very fit to keep up with the game.

- **Rule knowledge** – this is clearly the most important. If you do not know the rules of the activity you are in charge of, you will not be able to officiate.

- **Fair/unbiased** – officials in charge have to be neutral so that the rules are interpreted fairly for both sides.

- **Firm and decisive** – decisions have to be made quickly and precisely. Once made, they should be stuck to. There may be examples where assistant officials can advise, and a change of decision can be made, but officials must not give in to pressure from the participants.

- **Good physical condition** – eyesight and hearing need to be good. Officials in some sports also need to be fit – professional football referees have regular fitness tests which they must pass to be able to continue as officials.

❓ CHECK YOURSELF QUESTIONS

Q1 What would be the title of the senior official in charge of the following activities?
a rugby
b hockey
c volleyball
d gymnastics
e soccer
f cricket
g basketball
h tennis

Q2 What is the most important quality an official must possess?

Q3 What would be the most important piece of equipment a senior official at the following games would need to take on the pitch with them?
a rugby
b soccer
c hockey

Answers are on page 149.

Sports bodies and organisations

- All sport in the United Kingdom is organised through a network of sports bodies whose main aim is to increase the amount of participation.

- The major sports bodies include Sport England, UK Sport, the International Olympic Committee and the Central Council of Physical Recreation.

• Edexcel candidates do not have to revise this unit.

Sport England

- Until 1997, an organisation called the Sports Council was responsible for the overall organisation of sport. After that, it was replaced by separate councils for England, Wales, Scotland and Northern Ireland – the English one is known as Sport England. Three particular aims were identified for Sport England:

  • To get more people involved in sport.

  • To provide more places to play sport.

  • To present more medals through higher standards of performance in sport.

- In order to be able to improve the standards of sport, Sport England has established five national sports centres, which are centres of excellence. These are:

  • **Crystal Palace** (in London)

  • **Bisham Abbey** (in Buckinghamshire)

  • **Lilleshall** (in Shropshire)

  • **Plas y Brenin** (in North Wales)

  • **Holme Pierrepont** (in Nottinghamshire)

- The first three centres are multipurpose facilities offering swimming, tennis, gymnastics, soccer and athletics. Plas y Brenin particularly caters for mountain activities and Holme Pierrepont for water sports.

SPORT ENGLAND

QUESTION SPOTTER

A common question is to ask why centres of excellence have been established. You need to be able to give an example of one.

The Bisham Abbey centre of excellence.

 UK Sport

- UK Sport was set up by Royal Charter in 1996 with the general aim of leading the United Kingdom to sporting excellence and making it one of the world's top five sporting nations by 2012. This was to be done in the following ways:

  - By supporting winning athletes.

  - By supporting world-class events.

  - By establishing ethically fair and drug-free sport.

- UK Sport also administers the UK Sports Institute which is a network of nine regional centres. It works closely with Sport England to run campaigns such as Active Sport, Active Schools and Active Communities.

 International Olympic Committee

- This is the governing body of the Olympic Games. Its three main functions are:

  - To select the hosts for the Summer and Winter Games.

  - To approve all the sports to be included in the Olympics.

  - To work with the host city, international governing bodies and international sports federations to plan the games.

 Central Council of Physical Recreation

- The CCPR was founded in 1935 and deals with the 265 national governing bodies as well as:

  - acting as an umbrella organisation for national governing bodies and sport and recreation

  - acting to promote, protect and develop the interests of physical recreation at all levels

  - being at the forefront of sports politics, providing support and service

  - being completely independent of any form of government control

  - having no role or responsibility for allocating funds.

✎ Governing bodies

■ Each sport has its own governing body. The aims of each are:

- organising local and national competitions

- selecting teams for international competitions such as the Olympic Games, and the various World Championships

- keeping players and participants informed

- maintaining relationships with the media

- drafting the rules and laws of the game

- advancing the special interests of the sport.

England Netball is the governing body for netball in England.

CHECK YOURSELF QUESTIONS

Q1 Which centre of excellence would a high-level rower be likely to go to?

Q2 What are the two main aims of UK Sport?

Q3 What do the initials CCPR stand for?

Q4 Who would be responsible for setting the rules for a particular sport?

Answers are on page 149.

Amateur and professional sport

• Only students taking the AQA Specification A and B examination need to cover this session.

> **QUESTION SPOTTER**
>
> It is very common to get a question asking what the difference is between being an amateur and a professional sportsperson.

Definitions

■ Most sportspeople belong to one of these categories:

- **Amateur** – someone who takes part in sport, or an activity, as a pastime or hobby rather than for financial gain. They take part for enjoyment only, do not get paid and usually have a full-time, or part-time, job.

- **Professional** – someone who takes parting a sport, or activity, as a means of earning his or her livelihood. They get paid for taking part and do it as a full-time job.

■ There are also other types of sportspeople who do not fall neatly into the two categories identified above:

- **Semi-professionals** – these are people who have a job but also take part in some form of sport for which they get paid. They tend to have part-time jobs, which allow them some time to train and play their sport. Some have full-time jobs and play their sport during their leisure time.

- **Shamateurs** – this was an expression from the era where there was not as much professional sport as there is today. These people claimed to be amateurs but were, in fact, receiving illegal payments for taking part in sport.

- **Open sport** – this is where a sport enables both professional and amateurs to play and compete together. One common rule is that the amateurs taking part are not allowed to keep any prize money.

Golf is a major sport and often has open events such as the British Open.

⚏ Rule breaking

■ At one time, rugby had two distinct forms. The professional version was rugby league and the amateur form was rugby union. In 1995, the governing bodies decided to abandon the distinctions between them and rugby union officially became professional. Previously, rugby league players had been banned from playing rugby union because they were professional players who could not take part in an amateur sport.

■ Examples of the ways in which the rules were previously 'bent' include:

- **Sponsorship** – this is dealt with in more detail in Unit 17. Many benefits were gained through this.

- **Trust funds** – this is where money was paid into a fund that the competitor could not use while they were an amateur, but were allowed to use when they 'retired' from their sport.

- **Occupations** – many sportspeople had supposed jobs but were in fact allowed to take part in their sport nearly full time. This was very common in some countries for people who were in the armed, or uniformed, forces.

- **Scholarships** – many universities and colleges offered sports scholarships that effectively allow full-time sport to be undertaken – this was very common in the USA.

- **Expenses payments** – these were usually legitimate payments but the levels were falsely high, which would really amount to a full payment.

- **Illegal payments** – these were commonly known as 'boot money', a term that originated in rugby when players would find quantities of cash had been placed in their playing boots following a game.

- **Gifts** – these would range from prizes or gifts, possible even a luxury car, which could then be traded for money at a later date.

QUESTION SPOTTER

A common question is to ask for examples of the ways in which amateurs could get around the rules of not being paid to take part in their sport.

❓ CHECK YOURSELF QUESTIONS

Q1 What type of sportsperson gets paid for playing the sport and does it as a full-time job?

Q2 What is meant by an open sport?

Q3 What do you understand by the term 'shamateur'?

Answers are on page 149.

Competitions

■ The vast majority of sport involves some form of competition. This is one of the main reasons for taking part for many people.

■ There are various forms of popular competition.

🏸 Knockout competitions

■ Knockout competitions are played in rounds where two teams, or individuals, face each other and the winners go through to the next round until there are only two teams left to contest the final. This is a very common form of competition if there is a large entry, as you effectively reduce the number by half after each round.

■ Two good examples of this type of competition are the FA Cup in soccer and the Wimbledon tennis tournament. In the Wimbledon competition, the organisers make use of the 'seeding system' which gives the top players a particular place in the initial draw to make sure that they do not play each other in the early rounds. In the FA Cup competition, the top soccer teams from the higher divisions do not even enter the competition until the later rounds.

■ If you arrange a knockout competition it may be necessary to have preliminary rounds to make sure you have the correct number to take part. For example, 64 starters will produce 32 winners for the next round, then 16, then 8, then 4, then 2 before producing the winner.

Wimbledon is one of the most famous knockout competitions.

♟ Ladder competitions

- Ladder competitions are a popular form of competition in many clubs, especially those involving racket sports. All players have their names listed on a long 'ladder' and they have to challenge players above them on the ladder to take their place if they win. This means that the top players are at the top of the ladder and other players are seeking to get there.

- There are often rules about how many places above you are able to challenge, so it is not usually possible to move straight from the bottom to the top.

♟ Round robin

- In round robin competitions all the players, or teams, play against each other. It is only really suitable for a small number of entries because of the number of games that have to be played. It is quite popular with some tennis tournaments. The positive aspect is that all of the players get to play each other and it guarantees a lot of games.

♟ Leagues

- Leagues provide probably the most popular and common form of competition. Most organised sport has a league format. Here, teams are put into particular leagues and all teams, or players, in a league play against each other. Winning the Premier League Trophy is the aim of all the soccer clubs that play in the English soccer leagues.

- Matches are usually played both home and away and there is a promotion and relegation system where bottom teams go down a level and the top teams are promoted to a higher league. These leagues have to be arranged to take place over an extended period of time (usually the sports playing season).

- The advantages are a guaranteed number of games, advance notice of all games and fixtures, and also the most profit for many professional sports.

QUESTION SPOTTER

You might be given a particular sport, or a number of players, and then asked to suggest what the most appropriate form of competition would be.

Arsenal parade the Premier League Trophy to their ecstatic fans.

☌ Combined competitions

■ Combined competitions combine elements of all of the forms of competition explained above. They are very common in international competition. It is possible to play leagues as a qualifying method and then progress to a knockout stage as the competition reaches its climax.

■ Both the soccer and rugby world cups use this method, which has a qualifying league competition in its very early stage until the finals are staged over a period of a few weeks.

The Rugby World Cup is a good example of a combined competition.

■ These types of competitions are usually organised over a four-year period because of the number of teams that wish to take place and the number of games that have to be played.

CHECK YOURSELF QUESTIONS

Q1 Which would be the best form of competition for the following?
a forty soccer teams for a whole season
b six top level tennis players
c a small squash club
d sixteen badminton players for a half-day period

Q2 What is the main disadvantage of a knockout competition?

Q3 What format do the major international sporting competitions usually use?

Answers are on pages 149–50.

REVISION SESSION 4 — Facilities

■ In order for sport to be properly organised, there have to be the facilities for it to take place and the opportunity for people to use them.

> • Students taking the Edexcel examination do not need to revise this session.

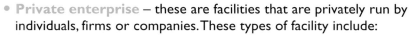 Providers of facilities

■ These fall into two main categories of local provision and national provision.

■ Local provision includes the following:

• **Local authorities** – these are the main providers and they will provide and maintain:
  – public parks
  – public playing fields
  – swimming pools
  – sports facilities in schools
  – local sports centres
  – local youth centre

Many swimming pools are dual use.

Swimming pools are one of the most common forms of local provision.

These facilities are usually jointly used by schools and local communities. They are open to all members of the public and used throughout the day, evenings and weekends – these types of facilities are therefore known as 'dual use'.

• **Private enterprise** – these are facilities that are privately run by individuals, firms or companies. These types of facility include:
  – health clubs and fitness gyms
  – hotels with sports facilities such as pools and fitness suites
  – holiday camps
  – riding schools
  – soccer and rugby stadiums and grounds
  – golf clubs
  – tennis and squash clubs

QUESTION SPOTTER

A common question is to ask what the difference is between the public and private sector in terms of sports facility provision.

To use these facilities, you usually have to become a member and pay to use the facilities, as they are run as profit-making concerns.

• **Private and voluntary clubs and associations** – these are not profit-making concerns, unlike the private enterprise ones. They include such things as local soccer clubs, bowls clubs and uniformed associations such as the scouts and guides. Some form of membership or payment is usually required, since the club or association must break even financially.

- National provision of sport and leisure facilities results from a combination of local and national funding. The agencies that provide funds include:
  - The Environment Agency
  - Countryside Commission
  - The National Trust
  - English Heritage.

- This area also includes those facilities provided by Sport England, UK Sport (see revision session 1) as well as national stadiums such as Twickenham, Wembley and Wimbledon.

QUESTION SPOTTER

There are often questions asking what factors should be taken into account when deciding where facilities should be located.

Factors affecting provision

- These are the factors that affect whether or not facilities are likely to be provided:

- **Population and expected use** – facilities are usually provided in more built-up areas close to larger populations to make sure there are enough people to use, and finance, them.

- **Access** – people need to be able to get to facilities by road, rail, plane, car, bus or even on foot!

Lakes are ideal for water sports.

- **Parking** – this is a priority as it is the most common way of getting to the majority of facilities.

- **Cost** – this can include the cost of the land to be used and the cost of constructing the facility.

- **Natural features** – in the case of many outdoor facilities this will be the main factor. Dry ski slopes are best suited to hillsides and lakes provide ideal bases for water sports.

- **Demand** – studies are usually made to establish whether or not there is a demand for particular facilities.

- **Competition and rivals** – there is no point in duplicating facilities as there is less likelihood that they will be fully used.

? CHECK YOURSELF QUESTIONS

Q1 What are the two main categories of provision for sports facilities?

Q2 What is a 'dual use' facility?

Q3 What is meant by public and private sector facilities?

Q4 Who would provide and pay for sports facilities in state schools?

Q5 Why are fewer facilities provided in more rural areas of the country?

Answers are on page 150.

UNIT 17: SPONSORSHIP

REVISION SESSION 1

Types and examples of sponsorship

> • Edexcel candidates do not have to revise this unit.

Who is sponsored?

■ Sponsorship is now an integral part of sport. It is available at all levels of sport, and takes different forms:

- **Individual sponsorship** – if an individual is sufficiently high profile and famous then sponsors will sign them up exclusively. A good example of this is Tiger Woods, the golfer, who is sponsored by Nike. Nike has even produced a complete range of Tiger Woods sportswear which bears a specific brand logo. Sports such as basketball, soccer and athletics are high-profile sports where the majority of the top-level performers receive individual sponsorship. This may be a performer's main source of income.

- **Team and club sponsorship** – at all levels of sport, clubs receive sponsorship. Local football teams might have the match ball provided by a sponsor. Top-level professional clubs enjoy greater amounts of sponsorship, even having their ground sponsored (as Bolton has with the Reebok Stadium). Not only will the team itself be sponsored, but individuals within the team will also enjoy the benefits that the sponsor provides.

- **Sports themselves, or the governing bodies** that control them, attract sponsorship. This is especially true if the sport has a very good image or is successful. Rugby attracted a great deal of sponsorship following the England team's win in the 2003 World Cup. This then meant that all the people involved in the sport nationally also benefited from it.

- **Sponsorship of events and competitions** – nearly all events are sponsored to some degree. The sponsors expect to have their names included in the competition or event. Who sponsors what is constantly changing as the organisers and administrators negotiate with different sponsors from time to time. For a very high-profile event, such as the Olympic Games, a lot of sponsors are involved. For something such as the London Marathon, there will be one major sponsor.

Tiger Woods is one of the top-level performers who receives individual sponsorship.

QUESTION SPOTTER

It is common to be asked to give an example of someone who is a high-level performer and receiving individual sponsorship. Remember that this is something that can change quite rapidly, so you need to keep up to date.

Flora sponsored the London Marathon in 2003 and 2004.

🎾 Types of sponsorship

■ Sponsorship now takes many forms:

- **Equipment** – a sponsor will provide all the equipment a performer needs, so that the performer is seen to be endorsing that particular company's products and brand.

- **Clothing** – like equipment, all the performer's sportswear, particularly their footwear, will be provided so that the brand name is given a high profile. This is one of the most competitive areas of sponsorship because of the size of the sports clothing and footwear industry.

- **Accessories** – performers are sponsored to wear items ranging from watches (worn by a tennis player on the serving arm's wrist so that it is filmed by the cameras) to sunglasses. Players may even negotiate deals for what they wear and promote when not playing the sport.

- **Transport and travel** – this can range from having a free car provided to being flown to different events by particular airlines. Even at lower levels, coach companies may arrange sponsorship deals.

- **Money** – a great deal of sponsorship is as simple as simply providing the performer with money. A performer is paid to be associated with a firm or company and promotes their sponsors through public appearances and advertising.

- **Training** – assistance with training is provided, sometimes through subsidising time off work to train or providing the equipment or facilities to allow the training to take place.

- **Entry fees and expenses** – these can mount up, so having them paid by the sponsor enables the performer to compete more.

- **Food** – sometimes a particular type of food is important, so this can provide a sponsorship opportunity.

QUESTION SPOTTER

Being asked to identify a particular type of sponsorship, and to give an example of how it can assist the performer, is a popular question.

? CHECK YOURSELF QUESTIONS

Q1 What individuals are sponsors likely to sign up to sponsorship deals?

Q2 How does a sport's image affect the sponsorship it may receive?

Q3 What accessories might a performer be sponsored to use? Give two examples.

Q4 Give an example of a sport where a performer may arrange a food sponsorship deal.

Answers are on page 150.

REVISION SESSION 2

Issues concerned with sponsorship

Acceptable and unacceptable sponsorship

■ Not all sponsorship is seen as suitable or acceptable. In some cases it is banned if the governing bodies do not approve of it.

■ Unacceptable types of sponsorship include:

• **Smoking and tobacco products** – because of the health risks associated with smoking, tobacco companies are banned from being sponsors. In the past, they were able to sponsor sports and events but this was gradually phased out. Motor racing is one sport where there is still some sponsorship from tobacco companies but government bans are being introduced to stop this.

Tobacco companies try to use sport as a way of avoiding bans on advertising their products.

• **Alcoholic drinks** – problems with alcohol abuse means that alcoholic drinks companies are not seen as suitable sponsors, especially for any form of youth sport. The governing bodies of many sports issue guidelines on how to prevent the sport being associated with alcohol.

• **Foods** – the issue of increasing obesity in young people has led to demands for certain fast-food companies to be banned from arranging sponsorship deals. Generally speaking, all other forms of sponsorship are seen as acceptable, mainly because sport is so dependent on the money it receives from different sponsors.

QUESTION SPOTTER

It is common to be asked for forms of sponsorship that would be seen as unacceptable. Tobacco and alcohol are the main ones you should consider.

Benefits for sponsors

■ Sponsors get involved in sport because of the benefits:

- **Advertising** – this is the main benefit for sponsors. Sponsors have large advertising budgets and since a great deal of sport is covered by the media, especially television, sponsorship is a good way of getting a company's product seen by millions of people. Advertising increases sales, and therefore profits, for the company. For tobacco companies, it is also a way around advertising bans on their products.

- **Image** – sport has a healthy, successful, positive image and it is a benefit for a company to be able to associate itself, and its product, with this. The company gains goodwill through helping out the sport and this helps to improve its image.

- **Tax relief** – companies are allowed to claim back a certain amount of the money they provide for sponsorship against the taxes they have to pay.

- **Research and development** – new products are tried out by sports performers to see how well they work.

CHECK YOURSELF QUESTIONS

Q1 Why is a tobacco company seen as an unacceptable sponsor?

Q2 Why are tobacco companies so keen to get involved in sponsoring sport?

Q3 Give the main reason why companies decide to become sponsors.

Answers are on page 150.

UNIT 18: THE MEDIA

Types of media involved in sport

■ As the media have grown and advanced technologically, they have become more and more involved, and influential, in sport. The main forms of media are television, radio, information technology and the Press.

> • Edexcel candidates do not have to revise this unit.

🎾 Television

■ Television is probably the most important area of the media in relation to sport. TV companies spend millions of pounds paying for the rights to broadcast major sporting events. Many TV companies have dedicated sport channels that broadcast only sporting programmes.

■ In the UK there are two forms of TV providers:

  • Terrestrial television – BBC, ITV, Channel 4 and Channel 5

  • Satellite and digital television – for example, Sky Television.

■ These companies broadcast a variety of different programmes that feature sport:

QUESTION SPOTTER

A popular question is to ask about the different ways that television covers sport.

  • live sporting programmes

  • highlights programmes

  • documentaries

  • quiz programmes

  • news bulletins

  • dedicated 'club' channels (these exist for some major soccer clubs)

  • educational programmes on school TV

  • 'magazine' programmes

  • text information services

  • interactive programmes.

TV companies have dedicated sports news channels.

🏸 Radio

■ Nearly all radio stations feature some sport in their coverage. Local radio stations cover local sporting events, while the national networks cover the major ones.

■ Like the TV companies, there are two main forms of providers:

- **Terrestrial radio broadcasters** – these broadcast on the FM, AM and medium wave networks and can be listened to on ordinary radios.

- **Digital radio broadcasters** – these can only be accessed through computers, satellite TV and DAB radios.

■ The growth in the number of ways in which radio stations can broadcast has led to an increase in the amount of sport covered. There are dedicated stations such as Radio 5 Live and TalkSport which cover the majority of the sporting events – often they cover events that some TV companies have not been allowed to because of the exclusive TV rights that some companies are able to negotiate.

■ The fact that people can listen just about anywhere, including getting a commentary at the event they are attending, makes radio very popular.

🏸 Information technology

■ IT is a rapidly developing and changing area of the media and sport is covered in a variety of ways, including educational, interactive, instructional and informative. All of the following forms have sporting links:

- computers, including laptops
- DVD and video
- mobile phones
- CD-ROMs
- the Internet.

Using the Internet to access information is one of the most common forms of IT use.

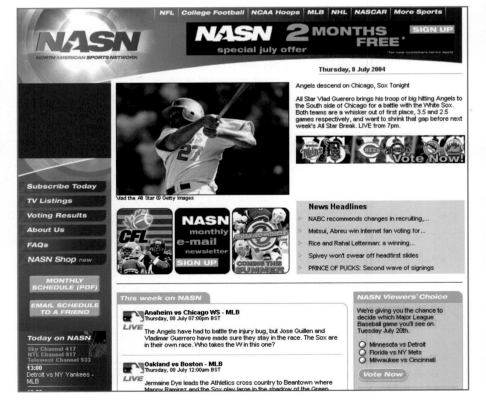

♟ The Press

- The Press includes:
  - newspapers
  - magazines
  - books.

- All these can be influential and informative in terms of their sports coverage. They have the added advantage of being very up to date in terms of news and developments. More and more specialist magazines are being launched and there are books published on just about every aspect of sport – especially educational ones linked to the study of physical education.

All newspapers cover sport in great detail.

☀ QUESTION SPOTTER

Questions asking how the Press can help to increase knowledge about PE and sport are common.

? CHECK YOURSELF QUESTIONS

Q1 Which is the most popular form of the media in terms of sport coverage?

Q2 What forms of television coverage are provided? Which is the most recent and rapidly developing?

Q3 What is the main advantage that radio has over television in terms of sport coverage?

Q4 Name two dedicated sports radio stations.

Q5 Which is the most rapidly developing and changing form of the media? How does it relate to sports coverage?

Answers are on page 150.

Issues surrounding media involvement

■ The media is very closely linked with sport. It is also very closely linked with issues surrounding sponsorship (see Unit 17). Because of this, media involvement has both positive and negative aspects.

Advantages of media involvement

■ Sport and the media would not be so closely linked if there were not a great many advantages to be gained:

- **Financial gains** – the broadcast media of television and radio have to pay to cover sport and events. The money involved runs into millions of pounds. All major events are televised and the companies have to bid for the rights to do so. The money is then paid direct to the sport, or event, and this can become the main source of revenue.

- **Raising profiles** – the image and profile of a sport can be raised if it is featured in the media. For example, there is a massive increase in the number of young people taking part in gymnastics immediately following the coverage of the event at the Olympic Games every four years.

Sports such as table tennis have their profile raised through media coverage.

- **Increasing knowledge** – the media are used as the main way of increasing knowledge of, and about, sport. Information is available through all the forms of the media so that people are more aware of sport and the issues associated with it.

- **Increasing participation** – one of the main aims of all forms of sport is to increase the amount of participation in physical activity or in a specific sport. Media involvement is one of the main ways of achieving this.

QUESTION SPOTTER

You may be asked how the involvement of the media can raise the level of knowledge about, and participation in, sport.

🎾 Conflicts between the media and sport

■ Just as there are great advantages to be gained from a high level of media involvement, there are also times when this can have negative effects:

- **Rule changes** – these may be introduced through media pressure, especially if they are seen as ways of making the sport, or event, more exciting or dramatic. Many of the rule changes introduced by governing bodies were suggested by the media – including the tie-break rule in tennis.

- **Undermining officials** – the use of instant replays can appear to make some officials' decisions incorrect, or unfair. Many sports are embracing the technology that the media can provide and using it to help with decision-making processes.

- **Intruding on events** – the presence of the media, which can include many TV cameras and large amount of cables and camera and sound operators, may get in the way of the spectator.

- **Timing of events** – the media may dictate the start time of an event to make sure it is broadcast during peak time in another country. Many events take place in the early hours of the morning to ensure that the largest TV audience can watch them live at a more suitable time in another part of the world.

- **Affecting the popularity or decline of certain sports** – if media coverage cannot be gained, then sports may go into decline. They may get too dependent on the money received and have problems if it is withdrawn.

- **Intruding on individuals' privacy** – the growth of role models in sport means that they lead a very high-profile life in the 'media spotlight'. Because of this, the media may intrude by following their every movement and judging their every action.

- **Discouraging attendance at events** – if it is known that an event is going to be shown live, then spectators may decide not to attend. Also, one event being televised may stop spectators going to other events or not taking part in sport themselves!

TV can show instant replays, which may undermine officials if mistakes are made.

> 💡 **QUESTION SPOTTER**
>
> Being asked to identify, and explain, the negative effects that media coverage can have on sport is a *very* common question.

❓ CHECK YOURSELF QUESTIONS

Q1 Which forms of the media pay the most money to be involved in coverage?

Q2 How can raising the profile of a sport increase participation?

Q3 Give an example of a rule change that was introduced as a result of media involvement.

Q4 Why might an event be staged live in the early hours of the morning?

Answers are on page 150.

REVISION SESSION 1

Increased leisure time

> • Edexcel candidates do not have to revise this unit.

Labour saving devices mean more leisure time.

■ The free time an individual has, when they are not working or at school, is leisure time. The amount available has increased in recent years because of the following:

• **A shorter working week** – in the past 40 years the working week has decreased from an average of 42 hours to a current average of 37 hours. This means more time is available for taking part in leisure activities. There are also greater holiday allowances and many people work part time or have shift work. This change in working patterns is the main reason for increased leisure time.

• **Increased automation** – machines are able to do jobs previously done by people; something as simple as an automatic washing machine makes more leisure time available.

• **Unemployment levels** – these are still quite high. People who are not able to find work have a great deal of spare time.

• **Earlier retirement** – people are generally living to a greater age but many are also taking up the option of early retirement.

QUESTION SPOTTER

A common question is to be able to identify the reasons why there is now more available leisure time.

Leisure and recreation provision

■ Recreation can be defined as taking part in a pleasurable activity. Many of the organisational sports bodies (see Unit 16) make provision for recreational activities. They also encourage active participation in sports.

■ Because there is now more leisure time, there needs to be increased provision for recreational activities:

• Sports – this includes leisure centres, swimming pools, ice-skating, etc. (see Unit 16).

• Cinemas, discos, clubs, ten-pin bowling, etc.

• Allotments, libraries, angling, cycling, etc.

CHECK YOURSELF QUESTIONS

Q1 What is leisure time?

Q2 What is the main reason for the increased amount of leisure time?

Q3 What is meant by recreation?

Answers are on page 151.

- Leisure and recreation providers have to cater for a wide variety of people in terms of age, ability and interest. Local authorities have a responsibility to make sure that the following user groups are considered:

  - **Unemployed and shift workers** – who may need daytime provision. It is for this reason that many leisure centres arrange daytime five-a-side leagues. They may also reduce their charges for unemployed participants.

  - **Parents and toddlers** – crèches are provided at leisure centres so that babies and toddlers can be taken care of while their parents take part in a recreative class such as an aerobic session.

  - **Retired people** – many sports centres arrange classes for the 50+ age group as well as for older people. Activities are tailor-made to be suitable for more elderly participants.

  - **Committed sportspeople** – many people want to take part in sport at a competitive level. These need to be catered for as well.

- Catering for the different needs of all these user groups is a complicated and labour-intensive business. It is one of the reasons why the leisure industry is the fastest-growing industry in this country and is rapidly becoming one of the largest employers.

> **QUESTION SPOTTER**
>
> You will often be asked to identify a particular category of user group that needs to be provided for by the leisure industry.

Bowls is an activity that is popular with senior citizens.

CHECK YOURSELF QUESTIONS

Q1 What particular considerations might providers have to make for the unemployed?

Q2 What specific provision would be useful for mother and toddler groups?

Q3 What special considerations need to be made for more elderly age groups?

Answers are on page 151.

REVISION SESSION 1

Historical issues

- Politics has always been linked to sport and probably always will be. Politics can both assist and interfere with sport.

• Edexcel candidates do not have to revise this unit.

QUESTION SPOTTER

Although it is more usual to be asked a question regarding how politics interferes with sport, there may also be one asking how it can assist.

How politics assists sport

- Politics can assist sport with:

  - **Finance** – the majority of funding comes from the government (see Unit 21).

  - **Organisation** – at the top of government there is a Minister for Sport and the government sets up the basic structures for the sports organisations (see Unit 16).

  - **Provision** – the fact that physical education is compulsory in schools (see Unit 22, page 124) was a political decision.

  - **Law making** – the standards for safety at sports grounds came about as a result of the Taylor Enquiry. This was set up after the Heysall Stadium disaster and the Hillsborough disaster.

  - **Raising the profile** – in the past, politicians completely ran sport in many countries. This happened especially in Eastern European countries such as Romania. Sport had a very high profile nationally and achieved a great deal of international success as a result.

  - **Supporting events** – major events, such as the Olympic Games (see Revision Session 2) cannot be staged without the help and assistance of governments.

The Hillsborough disaster led to rules being introduced for all-seater stadiums and crowd safety.

✎ Political interference

■ QUESTION SPOTTER

Questions often ask you to give examples of politics interfering with sport.

■ There are many examples of politics interfering with sport:

● **Political propaganda** – the most famous example of this is the Berlin Olympic Games of 1936 when Hitler used the games as a means of promoting his political beliefs.

● **Boycotts** – the Olympic Games of 1980 (Moscow) and 1984 (Los Angeles) were both subject to boycotts from some nations, because of the invasion of Afghanistan in 1979.

● **Terrorism attacks** – in 1972 the Munich Olympics were the stage for a Palestinian terrorist attack on the Israeli athletes. Security for all major events has been stepped up ever since because of this threat.

● **Apartheid** – the South African government introduced a law that segregated citizens on grounds of colour. In 1964 South Africa was expelled from the Olympic movement because of worldwide opposition. The law was eventually abolished and South Africa was re-admitted to the Olympics in 1992. The sporting ban on South Africa was thought to be one of the main contributing factors forcing the country to abolish apartheid.

The apartheid system in South Africa led to a ban on South Africans participating in world sport.

■ Sport has often been used as a political lever. Teams have been banned from playing, or touring, in order to bring political pressure to bear against their government.

❓ CHECK YOURSELF QUESTIONS

Q1 Which politician has overall responsibility for sport in the UK?

Q2 Which events led to the introduction of laws for the safety of spectators at sports grounds?

Q3 Which event sparked the boycotts of the Olympic Games in 1980 and 1984?

Q4 What is apartheid? Which country was banned from international sporting events because of its apartheid laws?

Answers are on page 151.

International sport and events

A common question is to ask what the advantages might be of staging a major international sporting event. You need to be able to give an example of one.

■ To compete at an international level is every competitor's dream. There are many major international events that are regularly organised:

• **Olympic Games** – these are the biggest of the worldwide events and are held every four years. They were re-started in 1896 and have been held regularly ever since, only being interrupted by the two world wars. There are now both summer and winter Olympics and countries have to bid to host them. Although it costs money to provide the necessary facilities, host countries make a great deal of money out of sponsorship and increased numbers of tourists. The 2004 Games took place in Athens, Greece, and the 2008 Games are scheduled for Beijing, China.

• **World Cups** – these now exist in the majority of the major sports in the world. Soccer, rugby, athletics and cricket have followed the example of the Olympics and stage their tournaments every four years, preceded by qualifying tournaments. The prestige of winning a World Cup is the aim of all the competitors and can raise the profile of the sport in the winning country.

The England teams won the Soccer World Cup in 1966 and Rugby World Cup in 2003.

• **Commonwealth Games** – these were based on the model of the Olympics and were started up in 1930 for all the countries that were members of the British Commonwealth. They are held every four years, following each Olympic Games by two years.

• **Specific events** – some sporting events have established themselves as major ones because of the reputation they have built up. These include such events as:

- Wimbledon – there is no official world championship for tennis but the Wimbledon Championship is considered to be the most important of the four Grand Slam tournaments, possibly because it is the only one played on grass.

- Boxing – many heavyweight contests attract a great deal of worldwide interest and are broadcast throughout the world with millions of pounds at stake for the television rights.

- The Superbowl is the climax of the American Football season and is billed as the world championship – despite the fact that only American teams take part! It arouses worldwide interest and is also televised live throughout the world.

Although the Superbowl involves only American teams, it is still seen as a major international sporting event.

■ If the media are involved, especially television networks (see Unit 18, page 107), it is possible to raise the profile of just about any event. Media coverage can turn a contest into a major international event and most sports are in the process of trying to achieve this. The first cricket world cup was not held until 1983 and the rugby one not until 1987, whereas the first soccer one was staged in 1930. It is likely that international sport is something that will continue to grow.

CHECK YOURSELF QUESTIONS

Q1 Which premier world sporting event has been established for the longest time?

Q2 How many years are there between the various world cup competitions?

Q3 Why are major events so dependent upon the amount of media involvement they can attract?

Answers are on page 151.

UNIT 21: FUNDING OF SPORT

 Local and regional funding

- Edexcel candidates do not have to revise this unit.

■ The finance and funding of sport is a complex matter that is closely linked with the various organisational bodies and facilities providers. (These are considered in detail in Unit 16.)

■ Sport is funded at local and regional level through clubs, charities, sport governing bodies and local government.

QUESTION SPOTTER

It is common to be asked how a small local club might be able to fund itself in order to continue to operate.

🎾 Organised clubs

■ There are a huge number of clubs in any particular area and they all have ways of raising money in order to exist. These are the most common ways:

• **Membership/subscription fees** – this is a set amount of money that each member pays to become a member of the club, or to remain as a member. Fees are often paid on an annual basis and can range from a few pounds for a local football club to over a thousand pounds for a golf club. On top of subscription fees, members may also be expected to pay match fees, which are a small sum of money paid each time they play.

Golfers pay quite a large membership fee to help to pay for the upkeep of the golf course.

• **Fund raising** – this can range from car boot sales, to raffles and social events; in fact anything the club can dream up to raise money.

• **Grants** – many small clubs receive grants, often from the local authorities to go towards their running costs.

• **Sponsorship** – this is likely to be very low level and could be as basic as having the match ball sponsored for a soccer club, or having free shirts provided with the sponsor's name on for a hockey club.

Charities

■ Many sports clubs are registered as charities. This means that they do not have to pay tax and they do not have to try to make money – only to break even.

Governing bodies

■ All sports have governing bodies. One of their main responsibilities is to provide some basic funding at local/regional level for people who want to take part in their sports. Money that the governing body is able to raise nationally is distributed to clubs to encourage the growth and development of the sport. A good example of this is tennis, as the profits from the Wimbledon Tennis Tournament are ploughed back into the sport at a local and regional level by the Lawn Tennis Association, which is the tennis governing body.

Profits raised from the Wimbledon tennis tournament are used to fund the sport locally.

Local government

■ Local authorities usually provide some facilities. Many sports clubs find this is too difficult for them to fund themselves. Clubs are then able to hire the facilities.

? CHECK YOURSELF QUESTIONS

Q1 Why would a member of a golf club expect to pay a much higher membership fee than a member of a soccer club?

Q2 Give two examples of how a small club might receive a form of sponsorship.

Q3 How might governing bodies raise money which they can then put back into sport at a local level?

Answers are on page 151.

National and international funding

■ At higher levels, sport tends to be mainly professional. This means that it is more expensive to provide but it is also more likely to attract higher levels of funding.

🎾 Professional clubs

■ All the major sports have professional clubs that compete against each other. The highest profile ones tend to be soccer clubs, but there is a growth in professional clubs in rugby, basketball and cricket. These professional clubs raise money in the following ways:

• **Spectators** – people pay for the privilege of watching professional sport and top clubs can attract tens of thousands of spectators. Large sums of money are raised through what is called gate receipts. Most clubs sell season tickets, which supporters buy in advance so that they can attend every home game in a season. These usually cost several hundred pounds.

• **Corporate hospitality** – another innovation is to provide executive or corporate hospitality boxes. These are designated areas that individuals or companies buy for large sums of money where they can watch matches in luxurious surroundings.

• **Merchandising** – top clubs have a variety of products for sale with their names and logos on. These products can range from the club shirt to clocks, pens and mugs. These are available to buy at the ground or stadium, or even in specialist shops which the clubs themselves set up. At least three top soccer clubs have their own dedicated satellite television channel which raises money for them.

QUESTION SPOTTER

Questions asking about the ways in which professional clubs are able to raise money are very common.

National Lottery

- The National Lottery (Lotto) is now one of the major ways in which sport receives funds. A percentage of the money received from the various draws is allocated to sport. In 2004 alone, Sport England (the organisation designated to distribute funding for sport) was responsible for distributing £108 million for community investment, £10 million for National Investment (money granted to 30 key sports) and £134 million for the Space for Sports and Arts scheme. Since the National Lottery started, it has contributed billions of pounds in funds to sport.

QUESTION SPOTTER

You may well be asked who distributes lottery funds to sport in the UK.

National government

- Some of the money raised through taxes is allocated to sport. The government also funds many of the national organisations such as Sport England (see Unit 16, page 93) and provides grants for many sports and organisations. If international events, such as the Olympic Games are held, then they are financed by the government.

The media and sponsorship

- The media and sponsorship need to be considered together in terms of funding as they are closely linked. Large amounts of sponsorship are available at national and international level because of the high-profile involvement of the media (see Units 17 and 18). Television companies will pay millions of pounds for the rights to televise certain events, competitions and tournaments; sponsors then also get involved so that their products can be advertised via the media.

- Sports authorities negotiate direct with the media and so do professional sports clubs – in many cases this is their biggest source of income.

The National Lottery is one of the largest funders of sport in this country.

CHECK YOURSELF QUESTIONS

Q1 State two main ways in which professional clubs can raise money.

Q2 Which body is responsible for the distribution of lottery money for sport in the UK?

Q3 Which area of funding is likely to be the largest contributor for most sports in the UK at national level?

Answers are on page 151.

Spectators and discrimination

 Spectators

■ At the majority of sporting events, the organisers encourage spectators to watch. In professional sport it would be unthinkable for an event to take place without anyone watching.

EDEXCEL CANDIDATES DO NOT HAVE TO REVISE THIS UNIT.

■ Spectators can affect sport in the following ways:

- **Financially** – spectators can provide revenue and finance for a sport or club, through paying an admission fee. However, spectators can also be an expense, as a lot of money has to be paid to provide security and safety. Whenever spectators are allowed to attend, facilities must be provided and the correct level of supervision and control must be in place. The police have to be notified, and trained marshals and stewards have to be present. The organisers must pay for this.

- **Influence** – it is generally accepted that playing at home gives a team an edge over the opposition. Not only are the home players familiar with their surroundings, but the crowd will be giving them full support and encouragement. For the opposition players, it is likely to be an intimidating environment as the majority of the spectators will be supporting the home team and not them. One of the most serious disciplinary actions which the authorities can take against any team is to make them play a game 'behind closed doors' – which means that no spectators are allowed to attend.

QUESTION SPOTTER

You may be asked a question about both the positive and negative effects that spectators can have at sporting events.

If there are large numbers of spectators, there will also be trained stewards to look after and control them. At some major sporting events, such as an important rugby or soccer match, there may be more than 60,000 spectators.

- **Behaviour** – there is a fine line between spectators being able to influence the outcome of a match through their vocal support, and their behaviour being so unacceptable that real problems occur. There are many examples of spectators invading the pitch, fighting rival supporters and even damaging the playing surface. In 1985, 39 people died at the Heysel Stadium in Belgium after fighting broke out between Liverpool and Juventus supporters and a damaged stand collapsed. In 1989, 96 people were crushed to death at the Hilsborough stadium when too many spectators were allowed into one part of the ground. These two disasters led to a complete review of crowd control and to the regulations being introduced that are in force today.

✏ Discrimination

■ **Discrimination** is defined as making an unjust distinction in the treatment of different categories of people, especially on the grounds of race, sex or age and it can exist in sport in the following ways:

QUESTION SPOTTER

You may well be asked a question about how discrimination has made it more difficult for certain categories of people to take a full part in sport.

- **Racial** – this may not only be in relation to the colour of someone's skin but also in relation to their nationality. The most extreme example of this was the apartheid system that existed in South Africa (see Unit 20, page 115). Laws have been introduced in the UK and America to make sure that this form of discrimination is not allowed.

- **Religion** – some religions do not allow events to take place on certain days. Some devout Christians refuse to compete on a Sunday. In many strict Muslim countries, religious rules forbid women to wear athletic clothing or swimming costumes so they are not allowed to take part in certain sports.

- **Gender** – sexual discrimination is something that is slowly decreasing. Longer-distance running events such as the marathon were considered to be too strenuous to include women – it was not until 1988 that it was finally included as an Olympic event for women. In some sports, such as netball, there are fewer events, less prize money and lower-profile competitions for female competitors. Women are not allowed to compete against men in the majority of sports – only show jumping and some other equestrian events allow men and women to compete on equal terms.

Sprinters Tommie Smith and John Carlos gave this 'Black Power' salute at the 1968 Olympics as a protest against racial discrimination in America at the time.

? CHECK YOURSELF QUESTIONS

Q1 How do spectators assist sport in a financial way?

Q2 What financial costs do spectators cause for sports clubs and organisers?

Q3 How might spectators influence a team or individual performance in a positive way?

Q4 What is meant by discrimination?

Q5 How might a person's religion affect their chance to take part in sport or sporting events?

Answers are on page 152.

School, peer and family influences on sport

🎾 School

- Since 1947, it has been a legal requirement for physical education (PE) to be taught in schools. The National Curriculum lays down guidelines about what should be taught to specific age groups of pupils. There are various ways in which pupils have an opportunity to experience PE:

  - **Timetabled lessons** – provide what is known as core PE. They are the set lessons which each pupil is expected to take part in.

  - **Extra-curricular** – these are other sporting opportunities, such as clubs, which may take place after school or at lunchtimes. They can include taking award schemes or being members of school teams or squads . They are voluntary so that no one is forced to take part – only encouraged!

  - **Exam-based courses** – these include courses such as GCSE and A level PE, or any other nationally recognised examination courses. These are offered by schools on top of the core provision.

PE is a compulsory subject that all pupils must take part in at school.

- The main reasons why it was decided that schools must provide PE were:

  - To improve health and fitness levels.

  - To provide a practical activity to balance many of the more theory-based subjects.

  - To prepare young people for a possible career in sport or physical education.

- For most people, school sport provides a basic introduction to sport.

💡 QUESTION SPOTTER

It is very common to get a question asking what benefits are gained through taking part in PE in school.

🎾 Peers

- Your peers are the people who are the same age and status as you. As a school pupil, your peers are the group, or friends, whom you associate with at school. The term 'peer pressure' means the ways in which this group can influence how you behave and act. Peer pressure can have the following effects in relation to sport:

  - **Positive effects** – if your peers are very positive about participating in sport and physical activities, it is likely that you will be influenced to take part too and that you will appreciate the benefits that can be gained.

  - **Negative effects** – just as peers can encourage you to take part, the reverse can also be true. It can be very difficult to ignore pressure from people who are trying to discourage you from taking part in sport – especially if they appear to be in the majority.

Family

- The influence of family, notably parents, can be a considerable one. Even before children go to school, they may become interested in a sport or activity through their parents and family. There are countless examples of children taking up the sport their parents excelled in.

- Generally, family influence is a positive factor on participation in sport:

  - Family members can assist with transport – for many young people being able to get to their sport or club can be one of the most difficult aspects.

  - They can provide financial assistance – this can be paying membership fees, buying sports clothing or providing specialist equipment.

  - They can provide support – many parents go along to support their children when they are taking part in sport. This encouragement can help to motivate a performance.

- In rare cases, families may have a negative effect by discouraging their children from taking part in sport.

QUESTION SPOTTER

A question might ask what influences families have on participation in sport. It would then be possible to consider either positive or negative factors or both.

Parents and family supporting young people while they play can be a motivating factor.

CHECK YOURSELF QUESTIONS

Q1 Why does every pupil have to take part in PE in school?

Q2 What is meant by 'extra-curricular activities'?

Q3 Give two benefits to be gained by taking part in PE in and out of school.

Q4 What is meant by the term 'peer pressure'?

Answers are on page 152.

EXAM PRACTICE

Exam tips

General tips

These tips apply to all the question formats for all of the specifications, regardless of the style of paper used by the exam board.

- Always read the question carefully. Look for information in it that is designed to help you. You can circle, or underline, key words in the question to help you focus. Be careful that you are answering the question that was set, not one you would like to have been set!

- Make sure that you have identified the 'command words': the ones written in **bold** type. Examples of these include:

  - **Give**, **state** or **name** – for these, a one word answer is enough. There is usually only one mark available, so do not be tempted to write a great deal as this will not give you extra marks.

  - **Describe**, **explain** or **consider** – these types of question require more lengthy responses. You need to give reasons in your answer. In structured questions, these question types appear towards the end of the question, as they are the most challenging and usually worth the most marks.

- Look at the number of marks available for the question, or the specific part of the question. You need to make sure that you include at least as many points in your answer as there are marks available, preferably more!

- Check if any examples are asked for – this is quite common in PE exams. Examples are often needed for questions asking you to describe, explain or consider. You need to use the examples to answer the question fully.

- If it helps you to answer the question more effectively, then draw a diagram. However, make sure that the diagram is clear and well labelled and do not use it as your full answer.

- Pace yourself! You will have a set amount of questions to answer and you must make sure that you answer them all.

- Specialist terminology will be used in the questions and you should use it appropriately in your answers. You must know exactly what the words mean.

- Check your completed answers and check again that you have answered all the questions and that your answers make sense.

- Practise answering papers before the examination. You will have improved your practical ability and mark by practising the physical activities in order to improve – adopt the same approach to the written paper. More practice is likely to improve your performance here too!

Specific examination board questions
Each exam board has a different format of paper:

- AQA Specification A has compulsory sets of structured questions with different sections to each question. The difficulty increases within each question, so the most difficult part is at the end.

- AQA Specification B has compulsory sets of structured questions with different sections to each question. The difficulty increases within each question, so the most difficult part is at the end. There is also a section with a choice of questions and in this section extended writing (essay type) answers are required.

- Edexcel has a paper which is divided into three parts. Part I has multiple-choice questions, Part II has short answer questions and Part III has scenario questions.

- OCR has short answer questions and structured questions that get more difficult.

When practising answering questions, you should stick to the format of questioning that your particular exam board uses and get used to that format – if you are not taking the Edexcel exam there is little point in practising answering multiple-choice questions.

Exam questions

Examples of the different formats are included here. Remember to check back on the format used by your exam board.

AQA Specification A
Structured question and student's answer

a The RICE principle is related to soft tissue injuries. **State** what the letters stand for:

R – _rest ✓_

I – _ice ✓_

C – _compression ✓_

E – _elevation ✓_

(4 marks)

b It is important when taking part in sport to warm-up properly.
Give two reasons why it is important to warm-up.

1 It is important to warm-up before exercise to allow the blood to flow much
faster around the body giving more to the muscles, ready for exercise. ✓
2 Also, it allows the muscles to stretch out and become prepared for the
exercise and strain that is about to be applied on the body ✗

(2 marks)

c If fatigue occurs it can affect a performance.
i What is meant by fatigue?

Fatigue is tiredness ✓ often caused by overuse of the muscles ✓ but it can
be caused by lack of sleep. When fatigued the athlete's muscles feel
very heavy.

(2 marks)

ii Give an example from a game activity and **explain** the effect that fatigue could have on the performance.

If a player was suffering from fatigue in a football match then that
player wouldn't be able to run at his fastest ✓ and his limbs would feel
tired and heavy and he would just want to relax.

(2 marks)

d Some activities, or sporting situations, are considered to be anaerobic.
i Explain what is meant by the term anaerobic

Anaerobic is when the body can do an activity without the need for extra
oxygen. ✓ The athlete does not need to breathe in any extra air.

(2 marks)

ii Give an **example** of when the body works anaerobically in a sporting situation.

✗

In a marathon race the runner has to take in lots of oxygen as they are going along to be able to keep their muscles working over this long period of time because it is going to take them hours to finish the race.

(2 marks)

iii Name the waste product that can be produced after working anaerobically.

✓

Lactic acid which is a mild form of poison which gets into the muscles and can leave you feeling stiff and uncomfortable if you do not cool down properly to get rid of it.

 10/15

(1 mark)

(Total 15 marks)

How to score full marks

a Full marks were achieved here but note that the question said state so all that was required was a one word answer for each. Do not be tempted to write more than is necessary.

b Answer 1 was correct and received the mark, but answer 2 just repeated the same point made in 1. A better answer would have been to refer to the fact that warming-up properly greatly reduces the chance of injury, specifically to muscles.

c i This was answered correctly and the marks were awarded for the first part of the answer. What followed was also correct but not necessary as the marks had already been gained.

ii The first part of the answer was correct but then the second part of the question, referring to effect on performance, was not covered. The point that the player would not be able to run at his fastest should have been developed to explain that this would then mean that they could not sprint back as defenders to cover attacks, or sprint into space if they were an attacking player. There should at least have been a reference to the fact that the standard of their performance would go down due to the onset of fatigue – a simple point such as this would have been enough to gain a mark.

d i There was not enough in this response to fully explain what anaerobic is, just one rather vague point made. A full definition would have been necessary, and more suitable. The answer should have stated that it is energy that is expended in short bursts, and that does not require oxygen. Alternatively the equation relating to anaerobic could be used, i.e. Glucose → energy + lactic acid, with the accompanying description regarding the short time it can be used for.

ii This response was incorrect because it is referring to aerobic, not anaerobic – a very common mistake. Therefore the example given was totally wrong, as was the rest of the response. A correct response would have referred to a sporting situation such as sprinting: a sprinter is required to perform in a short burst over a 100 metre distance and does not require oxygen to provide the energy to achieve this.

iii This response was correct but note that the question said name, so just writing lactic acid would have been sufficient – none of the rest of the response was required. It did not gain any marks and it was therefore not good use of time.

Overall, one-third of the marks were lost on this response because of poor exam technique, perhaps some lack of knowledge and failing to read questions carefully.

a   Fartlek, circuit, weight and interval are all types of training methods.
Briefly **describe** each type of training method
Fartlek
Circuit
Weight
Interval

(4 marks)

b   **Explain** what is meant by each of the following components of fitness.
i Muscular strength

(1 mark)

ii Muscular endurance

(1 mark)

iii Flexibility

(1 mark)

c   Cardiovascular fitness is required by many different types of athlete.
i What is cardiovascular fitness?

(1 mark)

ii Give an **example** of a sporting activity that requires a high level of
cardiovascular fitness.

(1 mark)

d   **Name two** socially accepted drugs, which are legal, despite having possible health
risks to those taking them.

(2 marks)

e   **State one** of the possible health risks associated with **each** of these drugs.

(2 marks)

f   **Name two** classes of illegal drugs that are among those banned by the
International Olympic Committee.

(2 marks)

(Total 15 marks)

Answers are given on page 153.

a Name **one** physical activity for which long arms or legs might be an advantage.

Basketball ✓

(1 mark)

b **i** Name **one** physical activity where suppleness is particularly important at the shoulder.

Gymnastics ✓

ii Name a different physical activity where suppleness is particularly important at the hip.

Gymnastics ✗

(2 marks)

c **i** What is glycogen?

It supplies stored energy ✓

ii Give **two** places in the body where glycogen is stored.

1 Muscles ✓

2 Heart ✗

(3 marks)

d **i** Carbon dioxide is one waste product of energy release. Name **two** others.

1 Water ✓

2 Heat ✓

ii How does the body get rid of waste products **during** physical activity?

By sweating out of the skin ✓ as the heat rises to the surface ✓

(4 marks)

e What is stroke volume? How does stroke volume affect performance?

Stroke volume is the amount of blood which leaves the heart with every beat. ✓ It affects performance by lowering the resting heart rate ✓ and this improves the performance. It also increases the oxygen carrying capacity in the blood. ✓

12/15

(5 marks)
(Total 15 marks)

How to score full marks

a Full marks were awarded here. You could also have chosen high jump, hurdles or volleyball.

b One mark was awarded for part (i) but the same activity was put in for part (ii) and the question asked for a different activity. Acceptable ones would have been hurdling, field event jumps, swimming, trampolining.

c Full marks were awarded for the correct definition given in part (i). In part (ii) muscles was correct but the second answer should have been the liver.

d Full marks were awarded. In part (ii) correct responses could also have included: by breathing/respiration and by urinating/excreting.

e The first part of the question was answered correctly as stroke volume was defined. In the second part of the question, only two more marks were given as only two points were made and a third one was needed for the extra mark. Additional, acceptable responses include: it increases cardiac output; helps reduce build-up of lactic acid; increases the capacity for aerobic production of energy; makes it easier to cope with exhaustion; improve stamina-based performance.

Structured question to try

a How are reactions measured?

(1 mark)

b Give **two** examples where fast reactions are important during a physical activity.
1
2

(2 marks)

c Dehydration is one condition that may occur as a result of physical activity. Name **three** others.
1
2
3

(3 marks)

d **i** What is meant by the training threshold?
ii How does age affect the training threshold?

(4 marks)

e Name **one** method of training suitable for anaerobic needs. Explain why it is suitable.

(5 marks)

(Total 15 marks)

Answers are given on pages 153–4.

Efficiency of the body systems is key to good health and fitness.
a How do the skeletal and muscular systems work together to produce movement for physical activity?

b How do the common injuries that can affect the skeletal and muscular systems occur? Give examples.

(a) The bones are held together by ligaments ✓ and the skeleton is a frame for the muscles to attach to. ✓ Muscles only pull, not push ✓ which is why they are arranged in pairs. ✓ The cartilage attaches the bones to the muscles ✗ and they help the muscles work in antagonistic pairs ✓ in the joints, which is where all movement occurs. ✓

(b) Common injuries which occur include tears, caused by sudden movements, ✓ fractures which could happen with an impact from a tackle. ✓ A sprain, which is a pulled muscle, ✗ or a strain, which is an overstretching of the ligaments at a joint, ✗ can also happen in games activities. If you don't warm up properly you don't get your muscles ready ✓ and you could also have problems if you don't cool down properly. ✓ If you don't wear protective equipment you could get a bruise if you were hit by a ball in cricket ✓ and you could get shin splints if you overdo it and stress your body. ✓

(12/15)

(15 marks)

(Total 15 marks)

How to score more marks

This question has been answered quite well, with at least 15 separate points made in the two parts of the question in order to attain the marks.

- In part a the comment regarding the cartilage was incorrect as it is the tendons that fulfil this role. A correct comment regarding the cartilage and its cushioning function would have obtained marks.

- In part b the comments regarding the strain and sprain were incorrect as they were the wrong way around! This is a very common error. If they had been the correct way around, two additional marks would have been obtained. Other answers that could have been given would have referred to accidental and deliberate contact with other bodies; the failure of equipment; deliberately disobeying the rules. All of these would need to have been linked with relevant examples of the type of injury which could occur as a result.

Extended writing question to try

1 Top sportspeople are always looking for ways to improve their performance.

a How can a sportsperson's diet help to improve their performance?

b How might the use of drugs affect performance? Give examples.

(Total 15 marks)

Answers are given on page 154.

Multiple-choice questions and student's answers

1 Answer questions by writing **A, B, C** or **D** in the spaces provided.

Fitness is:

A A capability of the heart, blood vessels, lungs and muscles to function at optimal efficiency

B The ability to meet the demands of the environment

C Training regularly

D A state of complete mental, physical and social well-being and not merely the absence of disease and infirmity

D ✗

(1 mark)

2 Which of the following statements describes a function of ligaments?

A Joins muscle to bone

B Helps support the joint

C Produces synovial fluid

D Forms a cushion between bones to prevent friction

B ✓

(1 mark)

½

(Total 2 marks)

How to score full marks

1 This candidate has answered **D** which is the definition of health. He has confused definitions and has not correctly identified the definition of fitness which was **A**. The other two choices are very vague, imprecise statements that did not apply to fitness.

2 **A** is tendons, **C** is the synovial membrane and **D** is cartilage.

Multiple-choice questions to try

1 Platelets are responsible for:

A Fighting infection

B Carrying oxygen

C Clotting

D Carrying carbon dioxide

(1 mark)

2 Which of the following statements describes the movements of the ribs and diaphragm during inspiration?

   A The ribs move up and out, the diaphragm moves down

   B The ribs move up and in, the diaphragm moves down

   C The ribs move up and out, the diaphragm moves up

   D The ribs move down and out, the diaphragm moves down

(1 mark)

(Total 2 marks)

Short answer question and student's answer

Answers are given on page 155.

The figure shows performers participating in physical activity.

(1 mark)

Complete the table below, naming **one** component of skill-related fitness that will be important to each performer. Explain how these components will help each performer in his/her activity. You **must** choose a different component for each performer.

Performer	Component of skill-related fitness	How component of skill-related fitness helps performance
A: Gymnast	Flexibility ✗	To be able to bend into difficult positions ✗
B: Sprinter	Speed ✓	To cover a short distance in a quick time ✓
C: Shot putter	Power ✓	To be able to combine speed and strength in a throw ✓

(6 marks)

How to score more marks

Part A for the gymnast was answered incorrectly as the component identified, flexibility, is not a 'skill-related' component but a health-related exercise component. The correct answer should have been balance, as this would have enabled the gymnast to retain their centre of gravity over the pommel horse as they completed their routine.

Short answer question to try

The **F.I.T.T.** principle is an important principle of training. Susanne is a hockey player and she has been applying the F.I.T.T. principle to her Personal Exercise Programme.

a   Complete the following statements about the F.I.T.T. principle by filling in the missing words.

   i   'F' stand for .... and means how often you train.

(1 mark)

   ii   **Intensity** refers to how ....you work when training.

(1 mark)

   iii 'T' refers to .... and means how long each training session lasts.

(1 mark)

   iv **Type** means that you should make sure that your training programme

   .... the activity you are training for.

(1 mark)

b   The following statements explain how Susanne has applied the F.I.T.T. principle to her training. Complete each statement.

   i   Instead of training once a week, she now trains .... times a week.

(1 mark)

   ii   Instead of working at 50% of her maximum, she now works at ....

(1 mark)

   iii Instead of working for 30 minutes per session, she now works for

   .... minutes.

(1 mark)

(Total 7 marks)

Answers are given on page 155.

Ashan is 16 years old. He is studying GCSE PE and has decided to measure his heart rate during training to help him monitor his fitness. The figure shows a record of Ashan's heart rate before, during and after a training session.

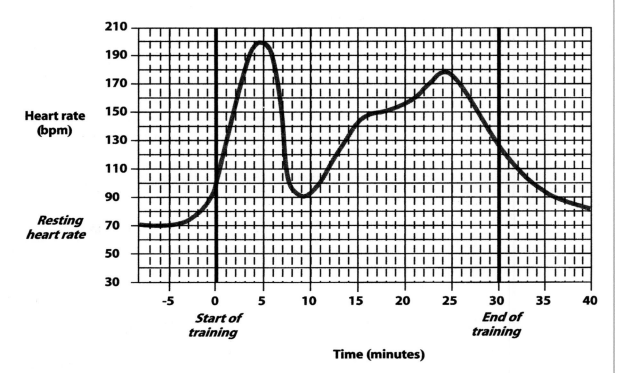

b i What happens to Ashan's heart rate **at the start** of the training session? (1 mark)

ii What effect will this have on his cardiac output? (1 mark)

c Explain why it is important to Ashan that his heart rate alters in this way. (1 mark)

d The graph shows that Ashan's heart rate varies during the training session. Give a possible reason for this variation. (1 mark)

e Name a type of **training method** that would cause this variation in heart rate. (1 mark)

f What happens to Ashan's heart rate during the 10 minute period after training has finished? (1 mark)

g Give **two** reasons why the heart needs to continue to work harder than normal, even after the training session has finished. (2 marks)

h At times Ashan is working well within his **target heart rate training zone**. What does this mean? (1 mark)

i Ashan is 16. Use this information to show how he would calculate his training zone by completing the following statements.

i Maximum heart rate is .... minus his age.

ii Therefore Ashan's maximum heart rate will be .... (bpm).

iii The upper limit of his target heart rate training zone should be

.... % of his maximum heart rate.

iv The lower limit of his target heart rate training zone should be

.... % of his maximum heart rate.   (4 marks)

j i Complete the statement below about the type of muscle found in the heart.

The heart wall is .... muscle.   (1 mark)

ii How does this type of muscle differ from voluntary muscle?

(1 mark)

k In addition to keeping fit, Ashan also knows that it is important to consider what and how much he eats.

Why would Ashan include the following in his diet?

i Carbohydrates ....……...………........   (1 mark)

ii Water ....……........   (1 mark)

l Why is it important that Ashan does not **under eat**?   (1 mark)

m It is important that Ashan does not over eat. Explain the term **over eat**.   (1 mark)

(Total 20 marks)

Answers are given on page 155.

Structured question and student's answer

a Anil notices that his heart beats faster when he begins exercise.
Why does Anil's heart beat faster?

Because his muscles need more oxygen ✓ ——————————— (1 mark)

b Briefly describe **one** test that Anil can use to measure flexibility.

Sit and reach ✓ ————————————————————————— (2 marks)

c Anil wants to improve his diet in order to have more energy when playing basketball. Use the table provided to help explain the types of food that Anil should eat in order to have more energy.

Food	Percentage energy (calories)		
	Carbohydrate	Fat	Protein
Porridge	54	33	13
Biscuits	51	44	5
Boiled potatoes	92	1	7
Spaghetti	85	1	14

Source: NCF Home Study Series – Nutrition Health Exercise and Sport (1995)

Carbohydrates will give him energy. ✓ _Fats give energy but he might put_
on weight. Spaghetti would be a good food for an endurance athlete. ✓ —— (4 marks)

d Anil wanted to improved his physical fitness. He decided to devise a Circuit Training programme.
i What is circuit training?

Going round and round in a circuit. ✗ ————————————— (2 marks)

ii Explain the advantages of participating in a Circuit Training programme.

You can do it to your own level. ✓
You can monitor your improvement. ✓
It works out different muscles. ✓ ————————————————— (3 marks)

e Anil is such a good basketball player that he was asked by a professional team to train with them. He found that the players always took part in a long warm-up before each training session.

Explain why performers warm up at the start of training sessions.

So that you can raise the temperature of the body ✓ and get yourself ready for the activity. ✓ It gets your heart rate up ✓ and your breathing rate as well, getting in more oxygen. ✓ The stretching exercises can help you to improve your flexibility ✓ and suppleness which is good too.

(6 marks)

(Total 18 marks)

13/18

How to score more marks

a Full marks were scored here. You could also have mentioned the fact that the blood carries oxygen and needs to be pumped around quicker.

b Only one mark was awarded because only the name of the test was given; there was no description. Mentioning that the feet need to be placed against the bench, that you have to reach forward slowly without bending the knees and measure the distance stretched past the heel would all have picked up extra marks.

c Three out of four marks were awarded. Mentioning porridge being a good all-round food or that biscuits are high in fat and therefore not ideal foodstuffs would both have gained the extra mark.

d i No marks were given because the answer was too vague and unclear. The student should have mentioned that it is a circuit if exercises are completed one after another and that you start at one point and then go around again, often several times and with rest periods. There should also have been some mention of repetitions and sets.

ii Three marks were awarded for three valid points made. You could also have mentioned that exercises can be changed to avoid boredom and given specific factors of fitness linked to the circuit.

e Five good points were made, which gained five marks. However, there was no mention of the warm-up preventing injury and this should have been mentioned for the final mark.

EXAM PRACTICE

a **i** What is a blister? (1 mark)

ii Describe the correct treatment for a blister. (3 marks)

b Beth takes part in a wide variety of physical activities. She uses different types of footwear for different activities.

Give the advantages of **three** different types of footwear used in physical activity. (3 marks)

c Beth was asked to organise a sports afternoon for her school. She was able to use the school tennis courts, the school gymnasium (Sports Hall) and the playing fields. Beth has to carry out a risk assessment on the facilities that are to be used.

i What is a risk assessment and how would Beth carry it out? (2 marks)

ii Give **one** different potential hazard that Beth may identify in **each** of the different facilities.

1 School tennis courts

2 School gymnasium (Sports Hall)

3 Playing fields (3 marks)

iii How does Beth minimise the risks that she has identified? (3 marks)

(Total 15 marks)

Answers are given on page 155.

UNIT 1: HEALTH AND HYGIENE

1 Health (page 3)

Q1 Use the World Health Organisation definition: 'A state of complete physical, mental and social well-being and not merely the absence of illness or disease'.

Q2 These include drunkenness, vomiting, lack of co-ordination, lack of balance and the slowing down of reactions.

Q3 This could really include any of the harmful effects listed on page 2 but the main ones would be lung cancer, heart disease and serious chest infections.

Comment Lung cancer would certainly be the most serious one.

Q4 Because it can prevent you from catching particular diseases that would be harmful.

2 Hygiene (page 5)

Q1 Because it is going to help to prevent the spread of germs which in turn helps to prevent your catching certain infections, diseases or illnesses.

Comment Linking this to a specific example, such as regularly washing yourself and your clothing, would be a better answer.

Q2 The most common ones are athlete's foot and blisters. Athlete's foot is a fungal infection between the toes. A blister is caused by constant rubbing of the skin. Either of these would make your foot area sore and uncomfortable, which would affect your ability to move easily. It could also mean than it would be difficult to wear the right footwear in the case of blisters on the feet.

Comment Whichever problem you choose as your example, it is important that you point out that it would cause your performance to be less effective.

UNIT 2: NUTRITION AND DIET

1 Basic nutritional needs (page 9)

Q1 Carbohydrates, fats, proteins, vitamins, minerals, fibre (roughage) and water

Comment Remember that fibre and roughage would be considered to be the same thing and not separate components.

Q2 The two types of carbohydrates are simple and complex. The three types of fats are saturates, mono-unsaturates and polyunsaturates.

Q3 This is the form in which glucose is stored in the liver and muscles. It is important because it is used as the main source of energy by the body when you are taking part in physical activity.

Comment Remember that when you are more active, there is going to be more demand for energy and therefore more demand on the release of glycogen.

Q3 To stop the runners becoming dehydrated through water loss. This could prevent them performing to their best or having to drop out of the race.

2 Specific diets for performers (page 11)

Q1 Diet 1: This would suit any type of endurance performer, such as a marathon runner.
Diet 2: This would suit a performer such as a gymnast or a jockey.

Q2 The two extremes are obesity, which is being extremely overweight, and anorexia which is extremely underweight. You could also include malnutrition, which means not getting the right foods to eat, and can lead to health problems. Severe malnutrition leads to very low body weight.

Q3 There are three times when you should not eat large quantities: firstly, just before activity, secondly, during the activity and, thirdly, immediately after the activity. In all three cases, the reason for not doing so is because your body will find it very difficult to digest the food as it coping with the demands of strenuous activity.

UNIT 3: HEALTH-RELATED EXERCISE

1 General fitness and exercise (page 13)

Q1 You could include any of the bullet points identified: improving body shape; helping to release stress and tension; helping you to sleep better; reducing the chances of getting illnesses and diseases; giving you a physical challenge to aim for; toning up the body leading to better posture; and increasing your basic levels of strength; stamina and flexibility.

> **Comment** There is no 'right' answer to this question – it will depend on what you would identify as the most valuable; all of the above would be acceptable.

Q2 You could include any of the bullet points identified: do not drive or be driven; walk at least part of a journey; use a bicycle; walk up stairs instead of using a lift; and do some simple stretching or flexibility exercise daily.

> **Comment** As in question 1, there is no 'right' answer to this question. It will depend on what you would identify as the most valuable and all of the above would be acceptable.

Q3 Any of the following effects would be acceptable: an increase in your pulse rate; an increase in your breathing rate; body temperature increasing and sweat appearing on the surface of the skin; skin reddening (especially on the face); a feeling of tiredness or heaviness in some of your muscles.

> **Comment** Make this a personal answer and refer to the effects that you have experienced yourself. As long as they are included in the list above, they would be acceptable.

2 Physical activity (page 15)

Q1 Because exercise in the form of physical activity improves health and fitness.

> **Comment** You only need to make a general statement. You do not have to point out all of the specific benefits of the five identifiable areas.

Q2 This is how the body weight is divided into fat and lean (muscle, bone, connective tissue and body organs). The figures are usually given as percentages.

Q2 The three factors are: your age, frame and sex.

> **Comment** All of the above are of equal importance and it is important that all three are given.

3 Specific fitness (page 17)

Q1 To be specifically fit, you have to prepare for the particular demands of the activities you are taking part in, which may be carried out at a high level. This is more than just having the general fitness of good health and being able to carry out everyday tasks comfortably.

Q2 You can do something about diet, drugs, weight and mental stress but you have no actual control over any physical handicap, illness, your height or somatotype.

> **Comment** There may be ways in which you can have partial control over some factors as you can adopt strategies to cope with stress and also take medication for some illnesses.

Q3 To get specifically fit for a marathon you would have to concentrate training on improving your endurance levels in terms of cardiovascular endurance and also muscular endurance. This would also include taking regular training runs of significant distances leading up to the overall marathon distance.

> **Comment** You could make reference to some specific training methods here but it is the emphasis on improving levels of endurance which is the key factor here.

UNIT 4: COMPONENTS OF FITNESS

1 What is fitness? (page 18)

Q1 Cardiovascular endurance – motor fitness
Muscular endurance – motor fitness
Speed – motor fitness
Strength – motor fitness
Flexibility – motor fitness
Agility – skill-related fitness
Balance – skill-related fitness
Co-ordination – skill-related fitness
Reaction time – skill-related fitness
Timing – skill-related fitness

2 Endurance (page 21)

Q1 The ability of the heart and lungs to keep supplying oxygen in the bloodstream to provide the energy to carry on with physical movement.

Q2 A performer with a good level of cardiovascular endurance has a relatively slow resting pulse rate and a quicker recovery rate when the heart rate returns to normal.

Q1 **a** Muscular endurance.
    b Muscular fatigue.

3 Strength (page 23)

Q1 The maximum force which can be developed within a muscle or group of muscles during a single maximal contraction.

Q2 **a** The greatest amount of strength that can be applied to an immovable object.

    b Muscular strength used in one short, sharp movement.

    c The strength a person needs to sustain their body over a prolonged period of time or to be able to apply some force against an object.

Q3 Because it is very difficult to measure strength; larger, better muscled people can often lift heavier weights but smaller people might have a better strength to weight ratio.

Comment *The main point here is that there is no standard way of measuring strength and that the greater the body size and bulk, the more likelihood there is that a heavier weight could be moved or lifted.*

4 Flexibility (page 25)

Q1 The range of movement around a joint.

Q2 Any stretching movement you usually perform could be included, such as a hamstring stretch, calf stretch or arm stretch. Remember that these only occur at the joints and the main ones are the shoulders and arms, back, hips and legs.

Comment *Describing a particular stretch that you regularly perform as a warm-up activity would be most appropriate. It is important not only to describe the stretch but also to be able to identify which particular muscle or muscle group you are stretching.*

Q3 So that the muscles are prepared for use, which minimises the chances of injury.

Q4 Any situation in which the increased range of movement has improved performance would be acceptable. This could be a hurdler who is able to clear the hurdles more easily, a gymnast who is able to perform more difficult moves or even a footballer who is able to stretch further to make a tackle or interception.

Comment *The main point needs to be that the level of performance is increased or improved, not just that the chances of injury are reduced.*

5 Speed, reaction time and power (page 27)

Q1 This is how quickly a performer can respond to something. A good example is a sprinter responding to the starting pistol at the start of a race.

Q2 Reaction time and movement time.

Q3 **a** These include inherited factors such as the number of fast twitch fibres you have and your body shape and size.

    b You could train to improve your strength and/or improve your technique by developing your action and style. You could also make speed work part of your training programme.

Q4 Power is the combination of the maximum amount of speed with the maximum amount of strength.

6 Co-ordination, agility and balance (page 29)

Q1 This would not be his dominant side so he would find it far more difficult as he would have a lower level of co-ordination.

Q2 This would very much depend on you as an individual and on the types of activities you carry out. Racket sports, in particular, need a great level of co-ordination, as you have to combine your body control with controlling a racket as well as controlling the ball or shuttlecock.

Q3 This is the combination of flexibility and speed and the ability to change the position of the body quickly.

Unit 5: Physiological and Psychological Factors

I Physiological factors (page 31)

Q1 Golf.

Q2 It is only in equestrian events (such as dressage, eventing and show jumping).

> **Comment** Just about all sports allow women and men to compete but not usually against each other. There are some examples where it has occurred in golf and there are mixed tennis matches. Remember that at school level no mixed activities are allowed where physical contact is permitted within the rules of the game, e.g. soccer and rugby.

Q3 This could be where their increased flexibility might be an advantage such as gymnastics or trampoline.

2 Psychological factors (page 33)

Q1 It can do both! A certain level will spur you on but if the level rises too much then anxiety may set in and the performance level might decrease.

Q2 Three factors would be: the enjoyment of taking part; keeping up their fitness levels; and getting a good score on their round of golf, possibly reducing their handicap for example.

> **Comment** Remember that intrinsic motivating factors are internal, personal reasons for wanting to do well.

Q3 Three factors would be: to win money; to win prizes/competitions; and the fame and glory associated with winning and being a successful member of their tennis club.

Unit 6: The Skeletal and Muscular Systems

I The skeletal system (page 37)

Q1 Support, shape, movement, protection and blood cell production.

Q2 **a** Long.
b Short.
c Flat, or plate.
d Irregular.

Q3 Immovable, slightly movable and freely movable.

Q4 A synovial hinge joint.

> **Comment** Note that the knee joint is one of the best examples of a synovial joint but it can also be referred to as a hinge joint as well.

Q5 Extension is where the angle between two bones is increased, such as straightening the arm at the elbow. Flexion is the opposite movement as it is where the angle between two bones is decreased, such as bending the arm at the elbow.

> **Comment** Another example is bending and straightening the leg at the knee.

2 The muscular system (page 41)

Q1 Voluntary (skeletal), involuntary (smooth) and cardiac.

Q2 The antagonist.

Q3

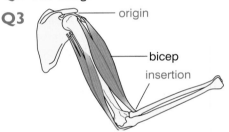

Q4 Slow twitch fibres, because these have a good oxygen supply and contract slowly, makes them more suited to endurance-type activities, of which cross-country skiing is one.

Q5 Biceps, trapezius, pectorals, gluteals, gastrocnemius, quadriceps.

Unit 7: The Circulatory and Respiratory Systems

I The circulatory system (page 45)

Q1 **a** The heart and blood vessels that carry blood around the body.

b The organs of the body involved in the inhalation and expiration of air.

c The circulation of blood and the transport of oxygen and nutrients to the cells of the body and waste products away from these cells.

Q2 Transport, temperature control and regulation, and protection.

Q3 The aorta.

Q4 a They carry oxygen to the parts of the body that need it.

  b They are the body's main defence against infection and disease as they produce antibodies to protect the body from infection.

  c These help with blood clotting and help to seal the skin and damaged blood vessels.

Q5 Veins carry venous, or deoxygenated, blood back to the heart, while the arteries carry oxygenated blood to the heart. The arteries are much thicker than the veins and do not have valves.

> Comment *The two main differences are which one carries oxygenated blood and the direction in which the blood flows relative to the heart.*

2 The respiratory system (page 49)

Q1 a The process that allows oxygen to be taken from the air and to be exchanged for oxygen.

  b Respiration with the use of oxygen, summarised as the equation Glucose + oxygen → energy + carbon dioxide + water.

  c Respiration in the absence of oxygen, summarised as the equation Glucose → energy + lactic acid.

Q2 The trachea.

Q3 In the lungs.

> Comment *A more precise answer would be to state that it occurs in the alveoli in the lungs.*

Q4 No, there is a difference, as the right lung is slightly larger that the left one.

Q5 The large muscle sheet that seals the chest cavity from the abdominal cavity and helps with the mechanism of breathing.

Q6 a Anaerobic respiration.
  b Aerobic respiration.
  c A combination of both.

> Comment *For the hockey player, short bursts of energy for sprints would be anaerobic and the endurance required to last throughout the match would be aerobic.*

Unit 8: Principles of Training

1 The five main factors (page 52)

Q1 a The particular kind of activity or exercise you use to build up or improve certain body parts or skills.

  b Making your body work harder than normal in order to make it adapt to improve.

  c Increasing the overload gradually and safely.

  d The loss of positive effects if you stop, or have to stop, training.

  e Making sure that you train to be ready for a particular event or activity.

Q2 If not all the factors are taken into consideration, any form of training undertaken will not be as effective, safe or beneficial possible.

Q3 Progression is moving forwards in your programme gradually and safely while overload is the way in which you are able to make this progression.

Q4 Although these might be specific to a particular programme you set up, there are standard safety areas which include: the use of equipment; movement of equipment; warming up and warming down; training partners (if weight training); wearing the correct clothing/equipment; care of the training environment.

> Comment *You should point out the safety issues that you have been able to specifically identify for your own personal exercise plan (PEP) as this is the most relevant.*

Q5 Because they would be training for possibly one particular event such as the Olympics and they would not be able to keep very high levels all the year round. They would train to peak for that one event in order to maximise success.

2 Practical applications (page 55)

Q1 a It prepares the body for the activity, raising the heart rate and breathing rate and stimulating the nervous system to get psychologically prepared. It reduces the possibility of injury, notably muscle injury.

b Activities should include: a continuous movement activity – often known as pulse raisers; light exercises – these would be targeted at certain muscle groups; and mobility exercises – stretches aimed at particular muscle groups and major joints.

Q2 This is in the fitness or exercise phase. Any example would have to reflect the particular training session you have chosen, such as concentrating on flexibility if it were a gymnastics training session (specificity) and increasing the time spent on one particular aspect (overload).

> Comment You should consider this question in light of your own particular PEP and how you included these principles in that.

Q3 This could be included for a specific activity-based session rather than a general fitness one to avoid tedium. Examples could include: dribbling a basketball around a set course, chest passes against a wall, continuous lay up shots, soccer ball dribbling.

Q4 These should be linked to the three areas identified: performing the training methods correctly; using the equipment safely; and using correct techniques.

> Comment Once again, you should link this to the safety considerations you have identified within your own PEP.

3 Planning, performing, monitoring and evaluating programmes (page 58)

Q1 Because this might show up any possible injury or health problems that would have to be taken into account. Also to be able to pitch the programme at the right level as all fitness levels will vary.

Q2 So you do not overwork particular areas or muscle groups but give them a little recovery time between exercises.

Q3 At the start you should always have a warm-up and at the end you should always have a warm-down.

Q4 To relieve the tedium and boredom that might set in if it is not both interesting and enjoyable. This would then lead to lack of motivation and not performing the programme well.

UNIT 9: TRAINING METHODS
1 Circuit training (page 61)

Q1 The principle of overload.

> Comment The principle of specificity would also be acceptable because you could set up a very specific circuit.

Q2 That activities are varied and similar ones do not immediately follow each other.

> Comment This is also so that muscles, or muscle groups, do not get over-used.

Q3 Firstly, to make sure that the correct technique is being performed. Secondly, to make sure they are being performed safely.

Q4 Fitness circuit – a general one working on particular aspects of fitness. Skills circuit – concentrates on including skills that might be used in a particular activity.

2 Weight, interval, continuous and fartlek training (page 64)

Q1 Strength.

> Comment It also helps to improve muscle tone, muscular endurance, speed, muscle size or bulk and can assist recovery after injury.

Q2 a The number of times you move the weights when training. If you were performing barbell curls and moved the weight up and down once, then it would equal one repetition.

b The number of times you do a particular weight activity, so each time you complete your repetitions of the barbell curls, you have done one set.

Q3 Isotonic is when the muscle contracts and works over a range of movement. Isometric is when the muscle contracts but in a fixed position.

> Comment The example of the bicep curl shows how the whole movement performed in one repetition is isotonic but if the movement is stopped at one particular point it is then isometric.

Q4 Interval training.

Q5 **a** Interval training (also probably some weight training).

b Interval training.

c Continuous training.

d Weight training.

e Interval training (also weight training to build up speed and power).

> Comment It is likely that all of the above would use a combination of methods, not just one. The particular one identified would be the primary one that is concentrated upon.

UNIT 10: DRUGS AND SPORT
1 Performance-enhancing drugs (page 67)

Q1 Drugs that performers take in order to improve their performance. Their use is banned by the ruling bodies of sport because they give an unfair advantage over other competitors.

Q2 To increase alertness, reduce fatigue and overcome tiredness.

Q3 Anabolic steroid.

Q4 **a** Martial arts and jockeys (and any other sports that have weight categories).

b Archery and pistol shooting (and any other sports that require you to be able to stay relaxed in terms of body movements).

Q5 Any endurance event such as long-distance running or the marathon as it increases your oxygen-carrying capacity and therefore gives you an advantage over other competitors.

2 Social drugs (page 69)

Q1 A socially acceptable one is one that is legal and can be of benefit. A socially unacceptable one is illegal and possibly harmful.

Q2 It could have a calming effect and so could be an advantage in archery, shooting and fencing.

Q3 A drug alters the biochemical structure. They are not all harmful and some may be prescribed to treat illness and injury.

UNIT 11: SAFETY AND RISK ASSESSMENT
1 General rules (page 71)

Q1 The ground could be too frozen and dangerous to play on. There might also be a risk of hypothermia if you are not dressed properly.

Q2 To make sure it is safe in terms of any dangerous objects being on it, such as glass, stones or damaged equipment such as the posts or flags.

Q3 Boots with studs in order to obtain maximum grip on the surface.

Q4 Because it could get caught in clothing and/or cause damage to the area where it is being worn. It could also injure somebody else if they were caught on it or struck by it.

> Comment This is a legal health and safety requirement and also applies in most workplaces.

Q5 Netball.

2 Activity-specific safety and risk assessment (page 74)

Q1 Any activity that allows physical contact within its rules.

> Comment The most common ones are rugby and soccer. It does not apply to hockey and basketball because the rules actually forbid contact although the reality is that it often happens!

Q2 All athletics events, rounders/softball, tennis.

Comment *Only activities such as hockey, rugby and soccer that have studded boots as the recommended footwear should be played in these conditions.*

Q3 Helmet, chest pad, gloves and protective footwear (kickers).

Q4 That there was a qualified supervisor in attendance.

Q5 Sudden rainfall could lead to the pothole flooding, trapping you inside.

UNIT 12: INJURIES
I Types and treatment of injuries (page 77)

Q1 **a** Strain.

b Sprain.

Q2 Simple (or closed), open (or compound) and complicated.

Q3 To support the area and apply a splint.

Q4 Ice.

Q5 Hypothermia is the rapid cooling of the body. Dehydration is a rapid loss of water from the body.

2 Basic first aid (page 79)

Q1 Do not move them.

Q2 Call for an ambulance or qualified medical assistance.

Q3 R = rest, I = ice, C = compression and E = elevation.

Q4 Injured limbs or wounds, such as fractures, dislocations.

UNIT 13: SKILL ACQUISITION
I How skills are learned (page 82)

Q1 Basic skills and complex skills.

Q2 Whole learning is when you perform the whole skill in its entirety. Part learning is where it is broken down into particular parts to be learnt separately.

Q3 To show them the correct way to perform the skill or movement so that they can then copy.

Q4 Input, decision making, output and feedback.

Q5 Where a skill learnt in one activity can also be applied in another one.

Comment *The examples of catching, throwing and passing are the best examples of transferable skills.*

Q6 A pole vaulter. The outdoor environment will affect the closed skills and the actual technique of the jump requires a high level of closed skills.

2 Feedback to improve skills (page 84)

Q1 **a** Intrinsic feedback.

b Extrinsic feedback.

c Knowledge of results.

d Knowledge of performance.

Q2 Just after the session has finished.

Q3 Identification of specific aspects of the performance that can be targeted for improvement in future practice sessions

UNIT 14: TECHNOLOGY
I Equipment, clothing and facilities (page 86)

Q1 Aluminium and graphite.

Comment *Titanium is also being used in some more modern rackets.*

Q2 Because the throwers were achieving such great distances that the stadiums were barely big enough and it was becoming dangerous for spectators.

Q3 They help with accurate line calls.

Q4 To reduce the drag effect of the water and so move through it more quickly.

Q5 To allow it to be used in all weathers so that it can be closed over in the event of rain.

2 ICT (page 88)

Q1 To help with decisions such as offside and whether the ball has crossed the line.

Q2 To carry out observation and analysis tasks on physical performances which can then help to make judgements about improvements.

Q3 Any form of athletics running events or activities requiring accurate timing to decide success or final placements.

UNIT 15: OFFICIALS
1 The role of rules (page 90)

Q1 Safety.

> **Comment** The other reasons listed would be important but safety would be the main one.

Q2 Temporary and permanent.

Q3 To be sent off from the field of play and excluded from the rest of the game.

Q4 This is not an enforceable rule but is the conventional way of behaving, showing fair play and good sporting behaviour.

Q5 They often apply pressure to make them happen so that sport appears more attractive and exciting.

2 Types of officials and their roles (page 92)

Q1 **a** Referee.

b Umpire.

c Referee.

> **Comment** In this sport, strictly speaking, it would be the first referee who sits above one end of the net with the second referee at the other end of the net.

d Judges.

e Referee.

f Umpire.

g Referee.

> **Comment** There is also an umpire but the referee is the senior official.

h Umpire.

> **Comment** For all of the above activities there are also assistant officials. The one named and identified is the most senior one.

Q2 Rule knowledge

> **Comment** This is the most important because all of the other ones depend on this being present.

Q3 In all cases it would be a whistle in order to control the play.

UNIT 16: THE ORGANISATION OF SPORT
1 Sports bodies and organisations (page 95)

Q1 Holme Pierrepont.

Q2 To lead the UK to sporting excellence and make it one of the world's top five sporting nations by 2012.

Q3 Central Council of Physical Recreation.

Q4 The sports governing body.

2 Amateur and professional sport (page 97)

Q1 A professional.

Q2 Where both amateurs and professionals can compete together.

Q3 Someone who claims to be an amateur but who receives illegal payments for taking part in sport.

3 Competitions (page 100)

Q1 **a** A league (probably broken down into two leagues of 20).

b A round robin.

c A ladder.

d A knockout.

Q2 Anyone who is knocked out in the first round does not get any more chances of playing any more games.

Q3 A combined system where they start off with qualifying leagues, then further leagues and finally a knockout stage.

4 Facilities (page 102)

Q1 Local and national provision.

Q2 One that is used both by schools and by local communities.

Q3 Public facilities may be used by anyone, but private facilities have restricted access. You usually have to become a member and pay to use these facilities.

Q4 Government and local authorities.

Q5 Because there are fewer people in rural areas.

UNIT 17: SPONSORSHIP
1 Types and examples of sponsorship (page 104)

Q1 Ones who are particularly high profile and famous.

Q2 If the sport or activity has a good image then the sponsors are more likely to want to be associated with them.

Q3 Watches (worn on tennis players' arms), sunglasses (often worn by cricketers).

Comment *There may be more current examples that you are able to point out from sportspeople currently taking part in sport.*

Q4 This could be an activity such as shot putt or discus where the performer needs to be quite bulky and have a high protein diet.

2 Issues concerned with sponsorship (page 106)

Q1 Because of the dangers and health risks associated with smoking.

Comment *In the majority of sports, smoking products are banned by the authorities.*

Q2 They are keen because it is a way around the advertising bans that are imposed on them.

Q3 Advertising of their product to increase sales.

Comment *There are other reasons but this is by far the most important reason why sponsors get involved.*

UNIT 18: THE MEDIA
1 Types of media involved in sport (page 109)

Q1 Television.

Comment *The other forms of the media do not have the amount of coverage that television has.*

Q2 The two forms are terrestrial and satellite/digital with satellite/digital being the most recent and rapidly developing.

Q3 It can cover more events, including local ones. It is not excluded by 'exclusive' deals that some of the TV companies are involved in.

Q4 Radio 5 Live and TalkSport.

Q5 Information technology – it can provide information, links to TV and radio, and also has educational, interactive and instructive possibilities.

2 Issues surrounding media involvement (page 111)

Q1 Television and radio, with television being the one that pays the most money.

Q2 The increased coverage means that more people see the activity being performed and then tend to want to take part themselves.

Q3 The tie-break rule in tennis.

Q4 Because the broadcaster wants to be able to broadcast it live to its biggest audience at peak time in another country in a different time zone.

UNIT 19: LEISURE AND RECREATION

1 Increased leisure time (page 112)

Q1 The time an individual has when they are not working or at school.

> **Comment** The change in work patterns would be the main reason and this includes fewer hours, shift work, longer holidays, etc.

Q2 The shorter working week and changes in work patterns.

Q3 Taking part in a pleasurable activity.

2 User groups and demand (page 113)

Q1 They might have to make daytime provision and also reduce their charges.

Q2 Childcare facilities such as a crèche for their children.

Q3 Tailor-made ones that would take into account the age factor.

> **Comment** An example of this would be to make them less strenuous and less physically demanding.

UNIT 20: POLITICS AND INTERNATIONAL SPORT

1 Historical issues (page 115)

Q1 The Minister for Sport

> **Comment** You should find out who currently has the position as it changes regularly.

Q2 The Heysall Stadium disaster and the Hillsborough disaster.

Q3 The invasion of Afghanistan in 1979.

Q4 A law that segregates citizens on the grounds of colour. It was introduced in South Africa, which was then banned from international sport.

2 International sport and events (page 117)

Q1 The Olympic Games.

Q2 Four years.

Q3 This is the main way in which they are made more popular and given a high profile. Finance consequently increases.

> **Comment** The link between popularity and finance is an important one. If the sport is popular then the media are more likely to get involved and inject finance in the running and organisation.

UNIT 21: FUNDING OF SPORT

1 Local and regional funding (page 119)

Q1 Because the costs of maintaining the golf course would be higher than those of maintaining the soccer club.

Q2 Receiving match balls for games or free sets of kit.

> **Comment** There are many other ways, e.g. providing transport such as minibuses or coaches.

Q3 Through organising and running major events in their sport, which in turn raises revenue.

> **Comment** You may be able to give examples of this; they include the tennis and rugby union governing bodies.

2 National and international funding (page 121)

Q1 Through spectators paying money to watch and through merchandising of products associated with the club.

Q2 Sport England.

> **Comment** Many clubs and organisations can apply for lottery money but it is Sport England that is given the responsibility of allocating it.

Q3 Sport England.

> **Comment** This is at national level, which you should not confuse with local level.

UNIT 22: SOCIAL FACTORS

1 Spectators and discrimination (page 123)

Q1 They pay to attend, which provides revenue.

Q2 Mainly security and facilities to make sure they are properly, and safely, looked after.

> **Comment** Particular aspects such as paying for a police presence can be identified, but it is security and safety that are the main factors.

Q3 They can support and encourage players, which can help them to do well.

Q4 Making an unjust distinction in the treatment of different categories of people, especially on the grounds of race, sex or age.

Q5 They might not be allowed to take part on certain religious days. They might even be prevented from wearing specific sporting clothing.

2 School, peer and family influences on sport (page 125)

Q1 Because it is a legal requirement.

Q2 Activities that take place out of normal school time such as lunchtimes or after school.

Q3 To improve health and fitness levels; to provide practical activity as a balance to more theory based subjects; and to prepare pupils for a possible career in sport.

Q4 This is the way in which your peers (groups of friends or people the same age as you) can influence how you behave and act.

> **Comment** Remember that peer pressure can be both positive and negative as it can encourage you take part as well as discourage you.

AQA Specification A
Structured question (page 129)

a Fartlek – speed training which alternates brisk walking, running, jogging and fast steady running
Circuit – exercises, or stations, arranged in a specific order which are all performed in turn
Weight – the use of free weights, or specialised machines designed to improve strength
Interval – periods of work followed by periods of rest which usually involves running or cycling

You would be awarded one mark each for each of these brief descriptions.

b i The maximum force which can be developed within a muscle or group of muscles during a single maximal contraction
ii The ability of the muscles, or a group of muscles, to keep working against a resistance
iii The range of movement around a joint

You would be awarded one mark for each of these correct definitions.

c i The ability of the heart and lungs to keep supplying oxygen in the bloodstream of the body to provide the energy to carry on with physical movement
ii An activity such as marathon running or cross country skiing

You would be awarded one mark for each correct answer.

d Socially acceptable drugs include nicotine and alcohol.

e There are various health risks associated with these:
Alcohol: drunkenness; vomiting; lack of coordination and lack of balance; slowing down of reactions.
Nicotine/Smoking: sore throats, nose and throat infections, headaches, dizziness, nausea and lack of concentration. Chest infections, heart disease, lung cancer, severe bronchitis and shortness of breath. Another problem is that smokers can endanger other people through passive smoking.

You would be awarded one mark for each of the problems correctly stated.

f These would include: stimulants; narcotics; anabolic agents; diuretics; peptide hormones, mimetics and analogues and blood doping.

You would be awarded one mark for each correctly stated class of drugs.

AQA Specification B
Structured question (page 131)

a By timing or measuring a response or by using a stopwatch / by the ruler test / by the speed of a response

You would be awarded one mark for any one of the above.

b Any two of the following list would be acceptable:
– reacting to the start of a race
– avoiding a punch in boxing
– avoiding a falling runner in a race
– adjusting position in response to a deflection
– tackling a side-stepping opponent in rugby
– intercepting a pass in netball
– goalkeeper making a save

You would be awarded one mark for each of the above.

c You could name any three from the following list:
– concussion/unconsciousness
– cramp
– hypothermia
– shock
– stitch

You would be awarded one mark for each correct answer.

d i The point at which training improves physical fitness; the maximum activity to bring about training effect or benefit; 65–85% of 220 minus age
You would be awarded up to a maximum of two marks for this part of the question.
ii Age affects the calculation of the training threshold formula; at a younger age the training threshold will be high; as age increases the training threshold will decrease.

You would be awarded a maximum of 3 marks for this part of the question and a maximum of 4 marks for the question overall.

e You could choose your training from any of the following training methods:
interval training, fartlek training, circuit training, weight training or even plyometric training.

Below are examples of how you could attain the 5 marks available for the explanation:

Interval training would enable you to work without oxygen (1 mark), and to improve your lactic acid tolerance (1 mark), this in turn would then extend your anaerobic work by delaying oxygen debt (1 mark). By using strenuous short bursts in your session (1 mark) this would also increase your metabolism (1 mark).

If you used circuit training this would mean that you could vary the intensity of your work (1 mark), the duration of your work (1 mark) and you could also vary the duration of your rest (1 mark). Using this method means that you could incorporate specificity (1 mark) and also that it would aid the removal of waste products such as carbon dioxide and lactic acid (1 mark).

Extended writing question

You would have to ensure that you answered both parts of the question to attain full marks. You could attain marks in the following ways:

a If a sportsperson has a good diet this would help to maintain their good health (1 mark), as they would be eating a balanced intake of the six food types (1 mark). They would need to avoid cholesterol-rich food (1 mark) and to make sure that they were keeping hydrated through a regular intake of fluids (1 mark). If they were a performer who needed a great deal of strength then they would need protein enrichment (1 mark) but if they were an endurance athlete they would support their stamina training through carbohydrate loading (1 mark). They could also help to support this stamina training through using fat as an energy source (1 mark) but they would have to make sure that they also maintained their body size, as they would not want to be carrying excess weight (1 mark).

This part of the answer has received 8 marks for the points made.

Marks could alternatively have been gained through referring to controlling diet when away from home, such as when competing abroad. You could also consider the timing of the food intake affecting performance, such as not taking meals just prior to a performance.

b Taking drugs could affect a performance either positively or negatively (1 mark). If a performer took steroids the this might help to build up muscle (1 mark) but it could also have dangerous side effects (1 mark), performers might also decide to take analgesics which would help the player to focus and mask any unwanted pain (1 mark) but this could just result in further injury (1 mark). In some sports beta-blockers are banned because they calm the nerves and reduce the heart rate (1 mark) but they can also have a bad effect by making you unable to respond energetically (1 mark).

At this point, 7 marks have been gained for part (b) which means that the 15 marks available for this question have been gained.

Marks could also have been gained for mentioning the positive and negative effects of diuretics, stimulants and social drugs but you would need to make sure that you referred to both the drug and its effect correctly.

If you had considered a performance effect in an appropriate activity, you would also have been awarded a mark.

You can achieve the maximum 15 marks by different routes, e.g. 9 for (a) and 6 for (b) or by 7 marks for (a) and 8 marks for (b) – but you must make sure that you answer each part.

Edexcel
Multiple-choice questions (page 133)
1 C, clotting.
2 A, the ribs move up and out, the diaphragm moves down.

Short answer question

a i F – frequency
ii I – intensity
iii T – time
iv matches / mirrors / reflects / is specific to / relates to or suits would all be acceptable.

b i Between 2 and 6 / more / several would all be acceptable.
ii 55–85% would be acceptable.
iii 31–60 minutes would be acceptable.

Scenario question

a The number of times the heart beats per minute
b i It increases.
ii It increases.
c It increases the blood flow / increases the oxygen supply
d Different work loads or intensities
e Fartlek or circuit
f It decreases
g 1 Retain oxygen debt
2 Help remove lactic acid
h The amount the heart rate should be kept within (the range)
i i 220
ii 204
iii 75–85%
65–70%
j i cardiac
ii Not consciously controlled
k i To provide energy
ii To prevent dehydration
l So that he has enough energy to compete
m Eating more than you need to eat for the amount of energy you are likely to expend

OCR
Structured question (page 138)

a i A bubble-like swelling on the skin usually filled with a watery substance
ii *Any of the following would be acceptable:*
– do not burst
– small blisters can be covered with a dressing
– ensure that the area is cleaned
– stop doing the activity that caused the blister
– seek medical advice

b *Any of the following would be acceptable:*
– boots – leather, studs for grip, ankle protection
– ice skates – high support, thin blade
– training shoes – light weight, good grip
– golf shoes – light weight, waterproof, small spikes
– walking boots – sturdy, waterproof, good grip
– cross trainers/running shoes – light weight

c i Risk assessment is looking for and identifying potential dangers / to performers, spectators and causes of injury. The following might influence it: preparation of the area; participation in the activity; equipment used and the environment.

ii 1 School tennis courts – the surface might be wet.
2 School gymnasium – the equipment might not be safe.
3 Playing fields – there may be litter or object pollution of the surface.

iii For the wet conditions that might mean that you are likely to fall over, or slip, you would not be allowed to take part on them if it was wet (1 mark). If equipment was not safe then it would either have to be repaired before use or you would need to buy new equipment (1 mark). If there was litter on the field which was dangerous, such as broken glass, you would have to get the ground staff or teachers to remove it (1 mark).

For part **iii**, you would have to make sure that it related back to part **ii** of your answer.

GLOSSARY

Aerobic respiration – respiration that uses oxygen

Agility – a combination of flexibility and speed and the ability to change the position of the body quickly

Amateur – someone who takes part in sport, or an activity, as a pastime or hobby rather than for financial gain

Amino acids – proteins in their digested form in the bloodstream

Anabolic steroids – performance-enhancing drugs that can increase muscle mass and help performers to train harder

Anaerobic respiration – respiration in the absence of oxygen

Arousal – the state of readiness of a performer

Articulation – the movement that occurs at joints

Balance – the ability to retain the centre of mass (gravity) of the body above the base of support

Basal metabolic rate – the amount of energy needed for important processes such as breathing and keeping the heart beating

Beta-blockers – performance-enhancing drugs that have the effect of calming and controlling the heart

Blood doping – a banned procedure that involves having a transfusion of blood to help improve performance in endurance-type events

Body composition – the percentage of body weight that is fat, muscle and bone

Carbohydrate loading (carbo-loading) – increasing the amount of carbohydrates in the diet to increase energy levels for endurance performers

Cardiovascular endurance – the ability of the heart and lungs to keep supplying oxygen in the bloodstream to provide the energy to carry on with physical movement

Cardiovascular fitness – the circulatory and respiratory systems working effectively together

Cardiovascular system – the circulation of blood and the transport of oxygen and nutrients to the cells of the body and waste products away from these cells

Cartilage – a tough form of tissue that covers and protects the ends of bones and acts as a buffer where two bones meet at a joint

Circulatory system – the heart and blood vessels that carry blood around the body

Closed skills – skills in an environment that does not change

Co-ordination – the ability to use two or more body parts together

Dehydration – rapid loss of water from the body

Diaphragm – a large muscle sheet that seals the chest cavity from the abdominal cavity

Discrimination – making an unjust distinction in the treatment of different categories of people, especially on the grounds of race, sex or age

Diuretics – performance-enhancing drugs used to increase the removal of water from the body at an accelerated rate

Dynamic strength – the strength needed to sustain body weight over a prolonged period of time, or to be able to apply some force against an object

Exercise – healthy physical exertion

Explosive strength – muscular strength used in one short, sharp movement

Extrinsic feedback – feedback received from sources other than the performer

Fitness – having a highly efficient body that can cope with a high level of physical demand

Flexibility – the range of movement in the joints

Gaseous exchange – the process that allows oxygen to be taken from the air and to be exchanged for carbon dioxide

Glycogen – the form in which carbohydrates are stored in the liver and muscles

Health – a state of complete physical, mental and social well-being and not merely the absence of illness or disease

Hygiene – making sure you are clean and healthy, and have good personal habits, to stop the spread of germs

Intrinsic feedback – feedback that is sensed, or felt, by the performer while they are performing

Isometric contraction – when a muscle contracts but stays in a fixed position

Isotonic contraction – when a muscle contracts and works over a range of movement

Joint – a place where two or more bones meet

Knowledge of performance – how well a performance was done rather than just the end result

Knowledge of results – also known as terminal feedback; the information you receive at the end of a performance

Lactic acid – a poison that is a by-product of exercise and that causes fatigue

Ligaments – strong fibrous bands that stabilise joints and control movement

Motivation – the amount of determination a performer has to do well

Movement time – how quickly a performer can carry out a movement

Muscular endurance – the ability of a muscle or group of muscles to keep working against a resistance

Muscular fatigue – the state of a muscle when it can no longer contract

Muscular strength – the ability to lift heavy weights

Narcotic analgesics – performance-enhancing drugs that hide the effects of illness and injury and that are used as a powerful painkiller

Nutrients – the substances that make up food

Open skills – skills used in constantly changing situations

Ossification – the process of development from cartilage to bone

Overload – making the body work harder in order to make it adapt to improve

Peaking – training to be ready for a particular event or activity

Peptide and glycoprotein hormones – performance-enhancing drugs that artificially increase the levels of hormones in the body

Physiological factor – one that affects your living body and therefore affects you physically

Power – the combination of the maximum amount of speed with the maximum amount of strength

Professional – someone who takes part in sport, or an activity, as a means of earning his, or her, livelihood. They get paid and do it as a full-time job

Progression – increasing overload gradually and safely

Psychological factor – one that affects, or arises in, the mind

Pulse rate – the rate per minute at which the heart beats

Reaction time – how quickly a performer can respond to something

Repetitions – the number of times you move weights when weight training

Respiratory system – the organs of the body involved in the inhalation and expiration of air

Reversibility – the loss of positive effects if you stop training

Sets – the number of times you do a particular activity when weight training

Skill – the ability to use knowledge or expertise to succeed efficiently and effectively in achieving a particular objective

Somatotype – body type

Specificity – particular kinds of exercises used to build up or improve certain body parts or skills

Sprain – injury to a ligament at a joint

Static strength – the greatest amount of strength that can be applied to an immovable object

Stations – the clearly laid out and labelled areas of a circuit used for circuit training

Stimulants – performance-enhancing drugs that increase alertness, reduce fatigue and overcome tiredness

Strain – injury to a muscle or tendon

Strength – the maximum force that can be developed within a muscle or group of muscles during a single maximal contraction

Tendon – fibrous tissue that joins a muscle to bone

INDEX

To my dearest wife, Louise. Without your support and patience this book would not have been possible.

William Collins' dream of knowledge for all began with the publication of his first book in 1819. A self-educated mill worker, he not only enriched millions of lives, but also founded a flourishing publishing house. Today, staying true to this spirit, Collins books are packed with inspiration, innovation and practical expertise. They place you at the centre of a world of possibility and give you exactly what you need to explore it.

Collins. Do more.

Published by Collins
An imprint of HarperCollins*Publishers*
77-85 Fulham Palace Road
London W6 8JB

Browse the complete Collins catalogue at
www.collinseducation.com

First published 2005

10 9 8 7 6 5 4 3 2 1

ISBN 0 00 719059 X

British Library Cataloguing in Publication Data
A catalogue record for this publication is available from the British Library.

Acknowledgements
The Author and Publishers would like to thank the following for their help in the preparation of this book:
Paul Kerr, Chris Taylor, Lorraine Franklin, Alison Clements, staff and students at Southfields Community College

The Author and Publishers are grateful to the following for permission to reproduce copyright material:
AQA: pp. 127-132; Edexcel: pp. 133-137; OCR: pp. 137-140

Photographs
Action Plus: p. 12, 50, 74, 76, 98, 125; Coloursport: pp. 91; 95, 110; Corbis: pp. 67, 115; Empics: pp. 10, 15, 16, 19, 21, 22, 23, 24, 25, 28, 29, 32, 45, 48, 49, 51, 59, 62R, 64, 65, 80, 85, 86, 89, 93, 96, 100, 102, 103, 104, 105, 111, 113, 116, 118, 122; Getty Images: p. 114; Mike Stuart: p.49; Paul Willatts: pp.10BL, 90; Popperfoto: p. 87; Press Association: pp. 26, 27, 31, 66; Rex Features: pp. 62L, 73, 81, 99; Roger Scruton: p.14; Sky Sports News: p. 107; Sporting Pictures: p. 117; Steve Lumb: pp. 19, 33, 55, 57, 60, 70, 72, 81BL/R, 82, 83, 84, 88, 124; Tony McConnell: pp. 71, 119

Illustrations
Jerry Fowler, Pat Murray and Sue Woollatt

Edited by Ros Woodward
Series and book design by Sally Boothroyd
Photo research by Thelma Gilbert
Index compiled by Julie Rimington
Production by Katie Butler
Printed and bound by Printing Express, Hong Kong

You might also like to visit
www.harpercollins.co.uk
The book lover's website